Lindemann Group
Peter Schiessl

Microsoft
EXCEL 2016
From the Beginning to Advanced Applications

Training book
with many
Exercises

ISBN 978-1-718185-05-0
Print on Demand since August 2018 in several editions
V250209 / Lindemann Group
Translated into English (US) by Peter Schiessl
Publisher: Lindemann BHIT, Munich
Postal address: LE/Schiessl, Fortnerstr. 8, 80933 Munich, Germany
E-Mail: post@kamiprint.de / Telefax: 0049 (0)89 99 95 46 83
© MSc. (UAS) Peter Schiessl, Munich, Germany
www.lindemann-beer.com / www.kamiprint.de

All rights reserved. Reproduction of separate pages, storage on data carriers, as well as any other use, such as the use of the book or the exercises in a computer course, if not every participant has acquired the book, require the written permission of the author.
Place of jurisdiction is Munich.

This book has been produced with the utmost care. However, due to the variety of software and hardware, neither the publisher nor the author can accept any liability for damage caused by errors in the book or the programs described.

All the mentioned names of programs are mainly registered trademarks of the respective manufacturers and are mentioned here only for the identification of these original programs, whose application is described in this training book.

This book was created using a standard installation of MS Office 2016 on Windows 10. Deviations from the descriptions and illustrations are possible through a user-defined installation, updates or other installed software.

Table of Contents

PART 1 7

BASICS 7

Windows Technics, Save, Input, Workbooks and Tables 7

1. Programs and Windows — 9
1.1 Excel Start-up 9
    1.1.1 The Quick Launch Toolbar.............................10
1.2 Entry in Excel...10
    1.2.1 The first Table 10
    1.2.2 Correct errors 11
    1.2.3 Completely replace Entry 11
1.3 Using the Commands..12
    1.3.1 The Icon Ribbon - a Multifunctional Bar 12
    1.3.2 Standard Actions to Open, Save, Undo..............12
    1.3.3 Icons example..13
    1.3.4 Command, Icon, or Shortcut 13

2. Save and Folders — 15
2.1 Extremely important Basic Knowledge...........................15
2.2 New Folder..16
2.3 Close File...17
2.4 Final Exercise 18

3. Workbooks and Tables — 19
3.1 What is Excel?..19
3.2 Different Database Calculation 19
3.3 The Workbook..20
3.4 Add and Delete Sheets...21
3.5 Rows and Columns 22
3.6 The Names of the Columns and Rows 22
3.7 Copy and Move..23
    3.7.1 Copy row 23
    3.7.2 Readjusting..24

4. The Excel Screen — 25
4.1 Quick Access Toolbar and Status Bar 25
4.2 Some important Icons..26
4.3 Sort the Columns 27
4.4 Format-Table 28
4.5 The Page View 29
4.6 Page Setup 30
4.7 Header and Footer, Page Setup 31
    4.7.1 Set up Header and Footer 31
4.8 Convert to Table 33
4.9 Summary 34

PART 2 35

CALCULATIONS IN EXCEL 35

Sum and other Formulas, copy formulas relative or absolute, the Formula editor 35

5. Calculate a Sum — 37
5.1 Preparation of the Exercise 37
5.2 The Input Options 38
5.3 The automatic Sum 38
5.4 Complete the Table 39
5.5 New Month, New Sheet, Rename 40

6. Formula and Coordinates — 41
6.1 Quick Entry by Pointing 42
6.2 Copy Formula 42
6.3 Insert the result with Sum 43
6.4 Absolute and Relative Coordinates 43
    6.4.1 Relative References 43
    6.4.2 Absolute References 44
    6.4.3 Copy Formula Absolute 44
    6.4.4 Replacements 44
6.5 Creating the Headline 45
6.6 Transfer Format 46
6.7 Room Calculation Exercise 47

7. The Function Wizard — 49
7.1 MegaMillions Numerary 49
    7.1.1 About the Categories 50
    7.1.2 The Help 51
    7.1.3 Add Formula 51
    7.1.4 Fix Results 52
    7.1.5 The Smart Tags 53
7.2 Depreciation 53
    7.2.1 Search Function 54
    7.2.2 Formula input by Pointing 55
    7.2.3 Copy Formula 55
    7.2.4 In conclusion 56

8. Invoice, Comment, Date — 57
8.1 The Numerical Formats 57
8.2 The Value Added Tax 59
8.3 A Comment 60
    8.3.1 Change Comments 60
8.4 Insert the current Date 61
    8.4.1 Calculations with Date 61
8.5 Rationalize Invoice 63

9. A Budgetary Planning — 65
9.1 Automatically Fill in with Row 66
9.2 Fill in automatically to the right 67
9.3 Document with Comments 68
9.4 Add Overview 69
9.5 The Expenditures 70

PART 3 71

CALCULATE INTEREST RATE 71

Financial calculations manually and with the formulas 71

10. Credit Calculation — 73
- 10.1 The Principle of the Calculation 73
- 10.2 The Calculation 74
- 10.3 The second Line 74
- 10.4 Completion 75
- 10.5 Count Rows 76
- 10.6 Values Vary 76

11. The Financial Formula PMT — 77
- 11.1 The Entry Menu 78
- 11.2 Explanations 78
- 11.3 The Function 79
- 11.4 Excel Credit Template 80

12. A Savings Bond — 81
- 12.1 Saved Amount 81
- 12.2 Determining the Saving Rates 82
- 12.3 Saving by Handwork 83
- 12.4 Help for the Formulas 84

PART 4 85

ADVANCED FORMATTING 85

With colors, frames, graphics and style sheets for professional excel sheets 85

13. Hide, Draw — 87
- 13.1 Hide 87
- 13.2 Drawing in Excel 88
- 13.3 Cell Styles 90

14. Styles in Excel — 91
- 14.1 A new Cell Style 92
- 14.2 Assign Styles 92
  - 14.2.1 Setting or Modifying Styles 93
  - 14.2.2 Complete Exercise 94
  - 14.2.3 Change Styles 95
  - 14.2.4 More about Styles 95
- 14.3 Advantages of Styles 95

PART 5 97
EXTENDED APPLICATIONS 97
A test evaluation with graphical representation of the result, Trend, SVerweis and more 97

15. A Series of Experiments — 99
15.1 Evaluation with Excel 99
15.2 Rounding..101
15.3 Copy Formulas...101
15.4 Error messages in Excel...102

16. Create a Chart — 103
16.1 As A New Sheet..105
16.2 Overview of Chart Functions......................................106
16.3 Add or delete Values 106
16.4 Final Exercise 108

17. Further Exercises — 109
17.1 A Travel Expense Accounting.....................................109
17.2 Currency Table 110
17.3 Score evaluation with VLOOKUP 111
17.4 Monthly salaries with Bonuses 113
17.5 Logic 115
17.6 Trend Calculation 117

18. Pivot Table — 119
18.1 Create Exercise Table...119
18.2 Overview of Formula Menu 122
18.3 Define Names 122

19. External Data, Monitoring — 125
19.1 External Data 125
19.2 Hide and Show..127
19.3 Formula Monitoring 128
19.4 Monitor Cells 129
19.5 Validation Rules 129

20. Index — 131

Part 1

BASICS

Windows Technics, Save, Input, Workbooks and Tables

General Abbreviations:

Files:	
[Ctrl]-s	Save
[Ctrl]-p	Print
[Ctrl]-f	Search
[Ctrl]-k	Insert Hyperlink
Date and Time::	
[Ctrl]-[Shift]-[;]	Insert Date.
[Ctrl]-[Shift]-[:]	Insert Time.
Undo, Copy:	
[Ctrl]-z	Undo
[Ctrl]-x, c, v	Cut, Copy, Paste.
Important Keys:	
[F1]	Help
[Esc]	Cancel, exit without changes.
[Alt]-[Return]	Force new Row in Cell.

1. Programs and Windows

1.1 Excel Start-up

> Click the Windows icon at the bottom left. Notice this:

- **Release the mouse button**, the start menu remains open and you can navigate through the menus with the mouse (without pressing!).
- Do not press again until the desired program is located.

Different programs are installed on each computer, therefore there are different start-up entries.

- **Excel 2017** is no longer located in the **Microsoft Office** folder, but directly under "**All Programs**":

Press the **Windows icon** once with the left mouse button, then in the second column, scroll through the **program list** to Excel at E.

You will find **Excel** directly in the program list under "E" in alphabetical order.

The most practical way to start is to add the Excel Start entry to the **Quick Launch bar**.

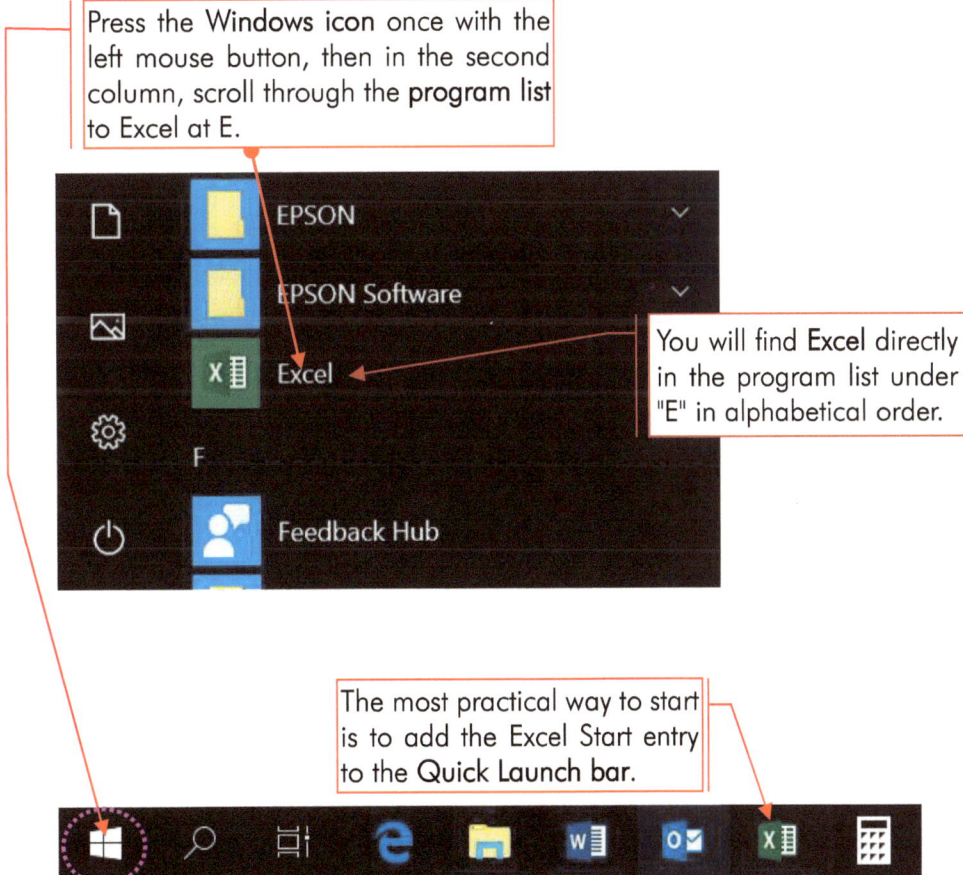

1.1.1 The Quick Launch Toolbar

If you work frequently with MS Excel, we recommend that you set up an Icon in the **Quick Launch toolbar**.

- The **quick start bar** is automatically activated in Windows; its entries are right next to the Windows Icon.
- Drag the Excel Start Entry (see the previous page) while pressing the left mouse button down into the Quick Launch bar next to Start.
  - Do not release the mouse until "**Link**" is displayed, otherwise, you are not yet in the correct position. Cancel with [Esc] if necessary.

An Excel-Entry in the Quick Launch bar does not interfere like a shortcut on the screen.

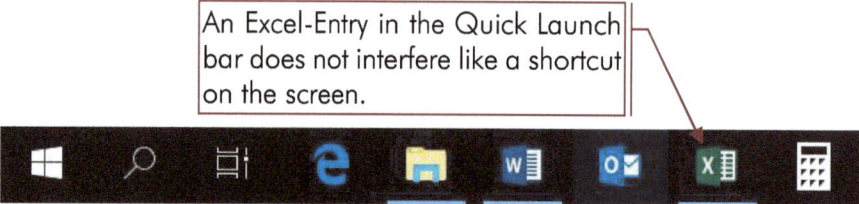

1.2 Entry in Excel

- Open **Excel** and select "**Blank** workbook":

- To other **Cells,** you will find
  - easiest method: click on the desired field with the **Mouse,**
  - with the **Direction keys,**
  - with **Return** or the [Tab] Key.

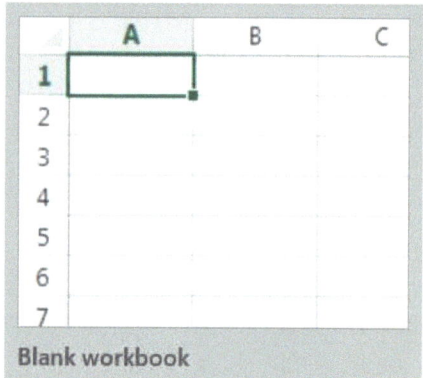

Blank workbook

1.2.1 The first Table

- **Enter** the following **Telephone directories** as your first table:

Walter	Walter	Building Services	222
Jeff	Norris	Administration	111
Ben	Wood	Distribution	232
Elisabeth	Newman	Administration	123
John	Kalman	Application	321
Nicole	Gaban	After Sales Service	254
Enter	Button	Computer System	214
Anastasia	Hampden	Distribution	253
Anton	Malham	Distribution	254
Anton	Pfefferson	Administration	287

1.2.2 Correct errors

You can click a cell and use the [Del] key to completely delete its contents. There are two ways to correct the content:

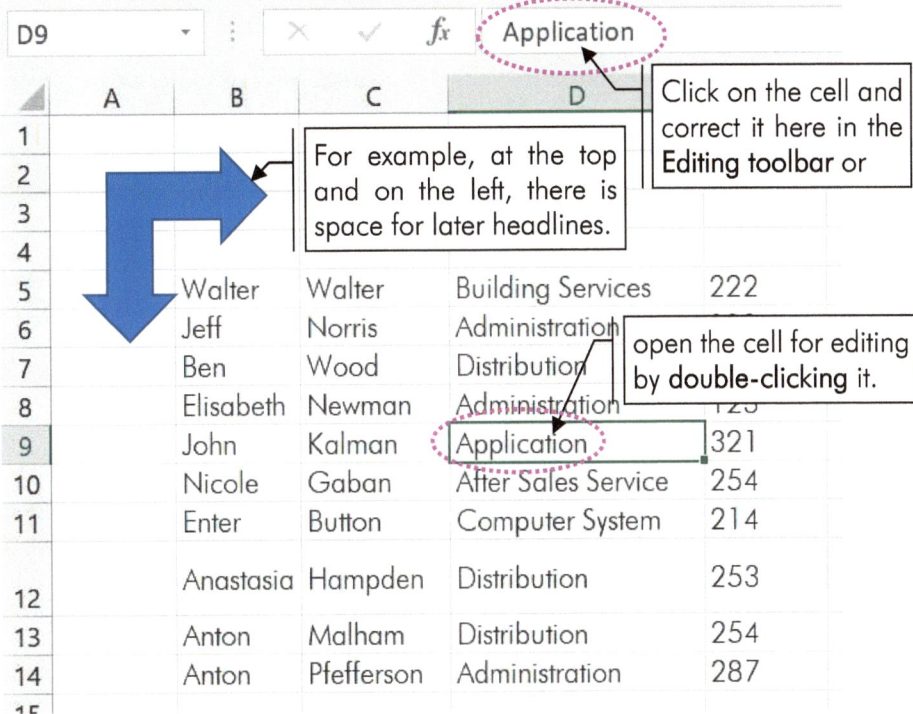

If the cursor blinks in the correct position (move the cursor with the mouse or the Navigation keys), you can delete it as usual with the [Back] key or the [Del] key.

Correct these:

> ➢ Walter Walter to Walter Smith and
>
> ➢ Computer System to Information Technology.

1.2.3 Completely replace Entry

To do this, it is sufficient to click on the relevant field once. The old text is replaced by the new text as it is written:

> ➢ Replace this: Enter Button to Ben Button.

> ➢ Delete Anton Pfefferson's entry completely. To do this, click on line number 14 on the left to select the entire line, then [Del].

Summary:

- ♦ to **Change** an entry, double-click with the mouse,
- ♦ click once to **Replace** and type a new entry,
- ♦ to delete, click once and press the [Del] key.

1.3 Using the Commands

1.3.1 The Icon Ribbon - a Multifunctional Bar

Excel offers many possibilities and settings. These must be made accessible to some extent.

- In the combined toolbar, most icons are sorted into groups (**tabs**: **Home**, **Insert**...):

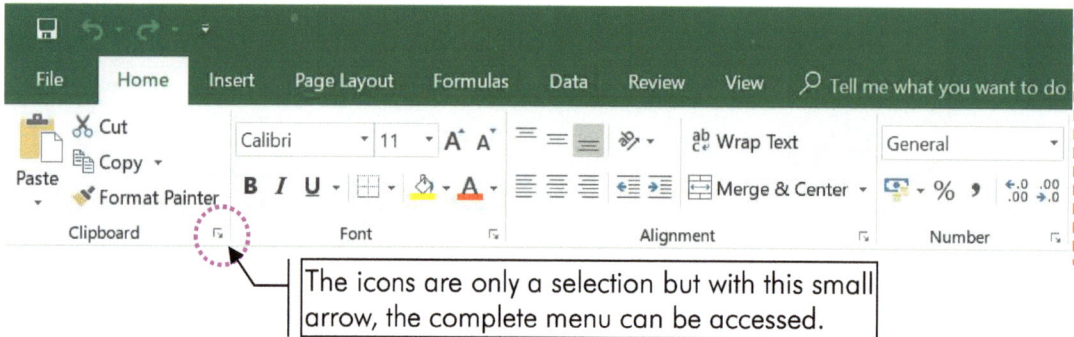

The icons are only a selection but with this small arrow, the complete menu can be accessed.

Depending on the width of the window, more or less caption texts can be displayed. In this respect, a large monitor with the highest possible resolution is therefore advantageous.

A first Overview:

- **Start**: Copy and Paste, Font and Paragraph Formatting...
- **Insert**: new Page, Table, Graph, Diagram etc. ...
- **Page Layout**: Page Format and Paragraph Settings ...
- **Formulas**: Insert Formulas or Date, Cross-references ...
- **Data**: Sorting, Connections, Filtering, Duplicates...
- **Checking**: Spell Checking, Protecting, Sharing...
- **View**: View type, Window, Macros ...

1.3.2 Standard Actions to Open, Save, Undo

Right above and under **File**, standard actions can be found:

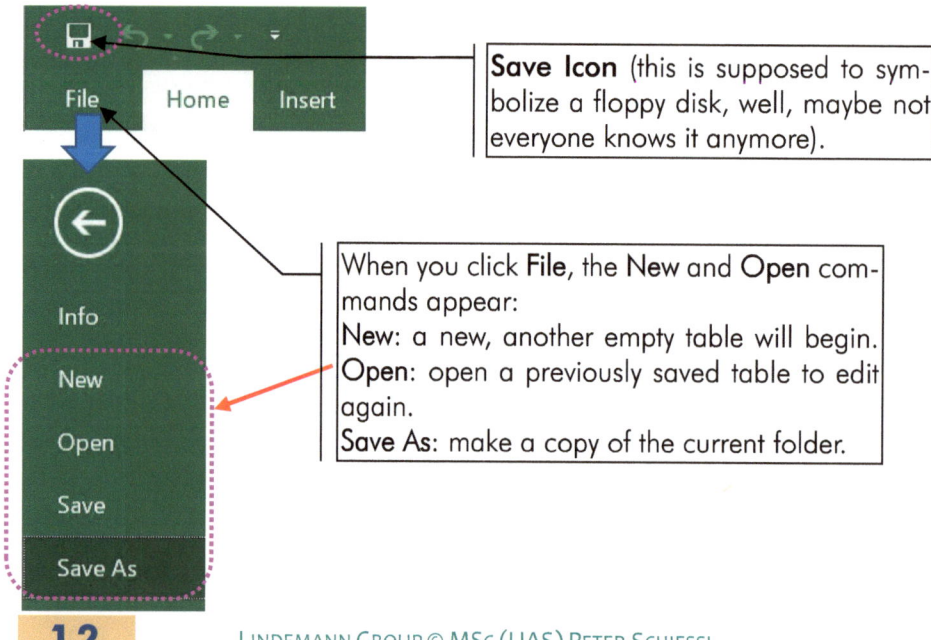

Save Icon (this is supposed to symbolize a floppy disk, well, maybe not everyone knows it anymore).

When you click **File**, the **New** and **Open** commands appear:
New: a new, another empty table will begin.
Open: open a previously saved table to edit again.
Save As: make a copy of the current folder.

1.3.3 Icons example

Select the correct **Filename** first, then **Start** to find icons and unroll menus:

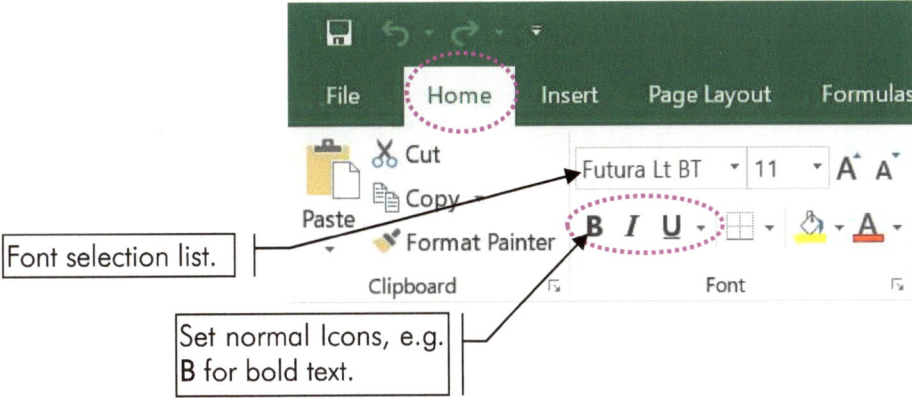

- **Information text** on the Icons:
  - Move the mouse over an Icon (do not click). After a short time, the system automatically displays what the symbol means.
  - If you move the mouse to the other Icons, their meaning is also displayed.
- Alternatively, **keyboard shortcuts** are available, e.g.:
  - **[Ctrl]-n**: start new File,
  - **[Ctrl]-o**: open existing file and
  - **[Ctrl]-s**: save the current work folder.

1.3.4 Command, Icon, or Shortcut

In the menu bar at the top, you will find all commands sorted, for example, all commands that affect the whole file, such as Open, Save and so on. Also, the Editing Bar in the File menu will be found below the Icon tape with the most important effects.

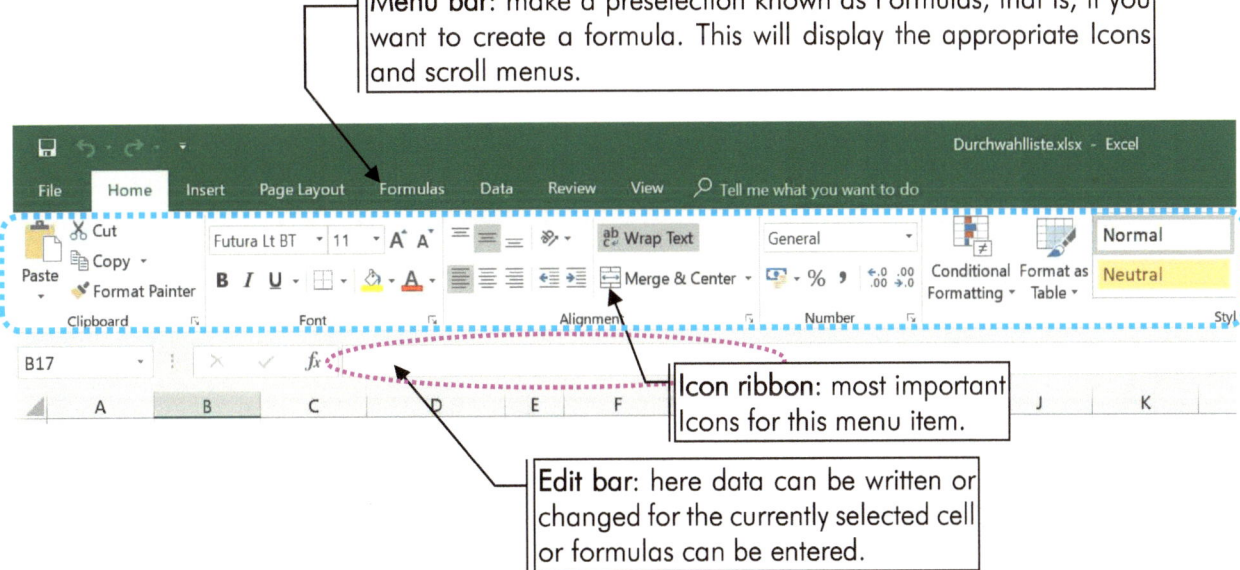

2. Save and Folders

There is usually a lot of work in a Spreadsheet (more precisely: Work folder). Therefore, it is time to discuss Saving.

- The data currently exists only in the **working memory** (random access memory = RAM).
  - This works electrically, so everything disappears as soon as the computer is switched off if we do not save it permanently on a **Data carrier**, e.g. on a **Hard disk** or USB stick.

2.1 Extremely important Basic Knowledge

- Each saved worksheet becomes a **File**.
  - Each file is given a **Filename** for differentiation.
  - **Filenames** can be up to 255 characters long.
  - Choose a file name that you can later use to identify the file in the best possible way.

- A **file extension** is automatically appended to the file name.
  - Based on this file extension, we can see whether it is a text (e.g. **docx**), a graphic (e.g. **cdr**) or an Excel workbook with the extension xlsx (formerly **xls**).
  - **File extensions** are not visible in Windows after a standard installation. In Windows 10, for example, you can activate them: in **Windows Explorer**, select "Change file and search options" and deactivate the "**Hide extensions for known File Types**" option on the View tab.

- An entire library can be stored on a tiny Hard Disk. This practically keeps the Overview, because,
  - files are sorted into suitable **folders**; such as conventional paper documents are filed in a folder with the appropriate label.
  - The same applies to the computer, that is why we will create a **new folder** for our exercise files before saving them.
  - Of course, a new folder will only be created once for a new type of files, e.g. a folder for our exercises or a folder for " Financing House Stonestreet 21 ".

> Please do not store thoughtlessly somewhere on the hard disk! After some time, you have a chaos of hundreds of files! It's hard to find files that were accidentally saved in the wrong folder!

2.2 New Folder

Let's save our phone list. But where to save?

- When saving for the first time, you will be asked for the **Filename** and the **location** (which data carrier, which folder?).
  - We want to save all Excel exercises, which we will create in the following and together in a **new folder**.
  - Therefore, we will create this new Folder in the first place.

This is very easy in both the **Save and Open Window**.

> Press the Save Icon (or [Ctrl]-s):

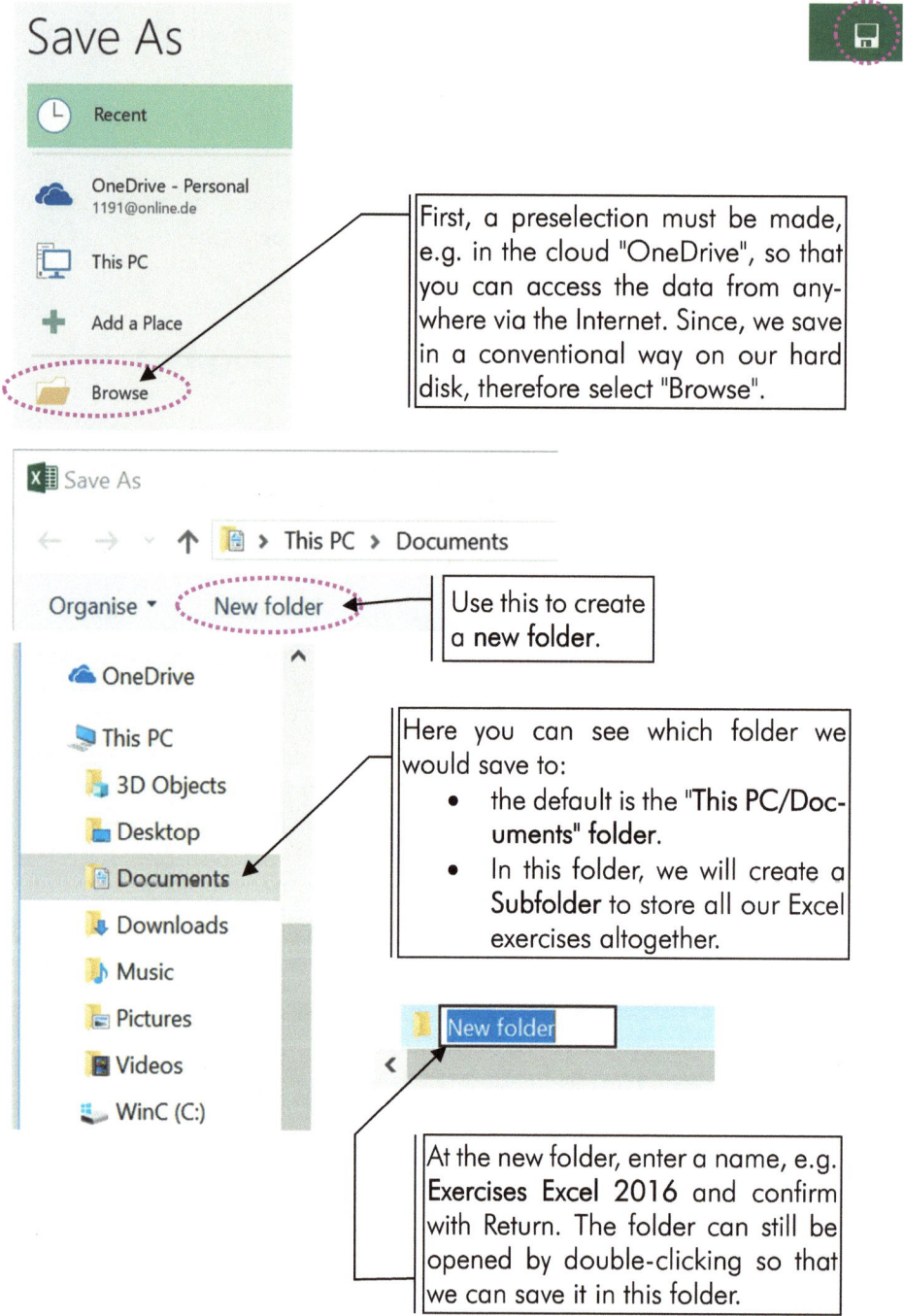

➤ Here the new folder "**Exercises Excel 2016**" is already opened by double-clicking and is displayed at the top so that the **File name** can be entered:

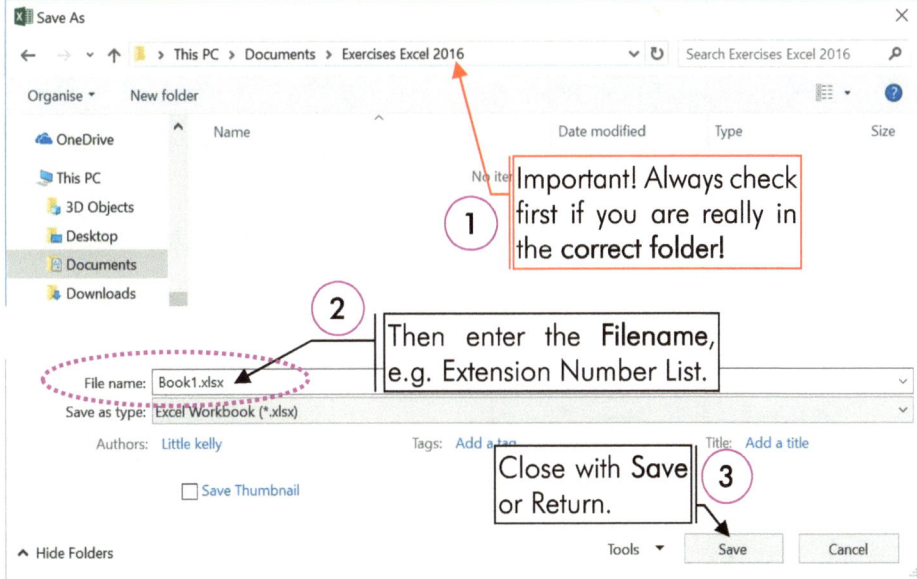

| Excel automatically adds the **File extension xlsx**.

2.3 Close File

What do you want to complete? The whole Excel or the current Phone Table?

♦ The ⊠-**Icon** at the top right is responsible for exiting:

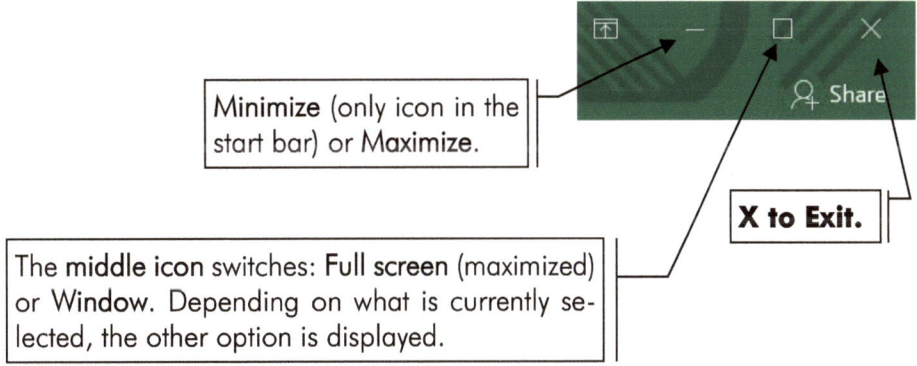

| Each **new worksheet** is opened in a new Window, with **[Alt]-[Tab]** you can easily switch between the Windows, or simply click with the mouse on the desired Window.

➤ **Exit** Excel.

2.4 Final Exercise

To routine an exercise for this basic substance.

Create File:

- ➤ **Create** another small Phone list.
- ➤ Save the list as " *Private Phone List* " in a **new folder "Phone Lists "** (always in our exercise folder!).
- ➤ Use **Save As** to create a backup copy on a USB stick with the name:

  Private telephone list with Current Date.

Window technology in Windows:

- ➤ Set Excel to **Full-Screen Size**.
- ➤ Start **Paint** (Paint 3D) with a new Drawing.
- ➤ Switch to Excel ([Alt]-[Tab]).
- ➤ Position both Excel and Paint so that Paint is on the left and Excel on the right.
- ➤ Right Mouse Button in the free area of the Start Bar and select **Overlapping**.

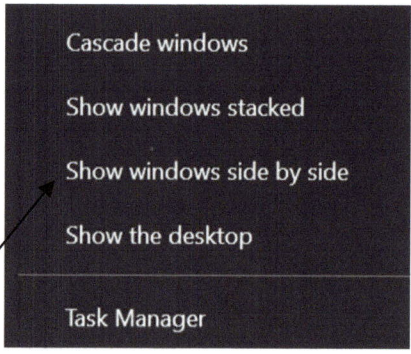

> **Try Cascade windows, stacked and side by side**. Display desktop reduces all programs to one Icon in the start bar.

Window technology in Excel:

- ➤ Exit Paint, set Excel to full screen and also open the first Phone List.
- ➤ Arrange the two telephone lists as follows: one at the top, the other at the bottom (first make the window smaller).
- ➤ Switch both lists to full screen and switch to another Phone list for **View/Switch Windows**.
- ➤ In Excel, choose **View/Arrange All**:

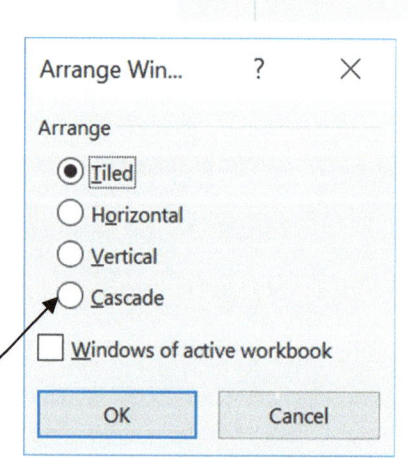

> Try it out, too. For example, if two folders are open, you can arrange them horizontally, that is, below each other to copy from one folder to the other. Alternatively, in a vertical Position (= next to each other).

- ➤ **Exit** Excel.

3. Workbooks and Tables

The phone list in the previous chapter explained a lot. Here is an overview of Excel with the first formula based on an exercise.

3.1 What is Excel?

Excel is a so-called **Table-Calculation-Program**. This means that we can enter Data and have Calculations carried out automatically, e.g. for an Invoice:

Items	E-Price	Quant.	Price
Pencils	0,99	3	2,97 €
Eraser	2,50	2	5,00 €
		Total::	7,97 €

So that Excel recognizes which data belong to the same **table** (see example), hence the name **Spreadsheet**.

Small Overview:

- **Operating system:** Windows, Linux, Unix, Apple IOS, Android ...
- **Word processing:** MS Word, Open Office Writer, Corel WordPerfect...
- **Spreadsheet:** Excel, Lotus 1 2 3, Libre Office Calc, PlanMaker, Numbers...
- **Database:** Access, dBase, FoxPro, MySQL ...

3.2 Different Database Calculation

The following classification is intended to illustrate the difference between a Database and a Calculation Program:

- In a **Database program** (e.g. MS Access) **Data** (addresses, telephone numbers...) are mainly collected in order to use them, e.g. for serial letters.

- In a **calculation program** (e.g. Excel), **calculations** should mainly be carried out, such as sales overviews, Invoices, Statistics, Evaluations, comparison leasing or purchase etc.

3.3 The Workbook

For instance, the data will be entered in a **Table** to ensure that Excel knows which values are to be added.

Since several calculations often belong to a project, multiple Tables can be created in one **Workbook**. The separate Tables are called **Sheets**.

Sheets

➢ **Open** the practice text for Phone List.

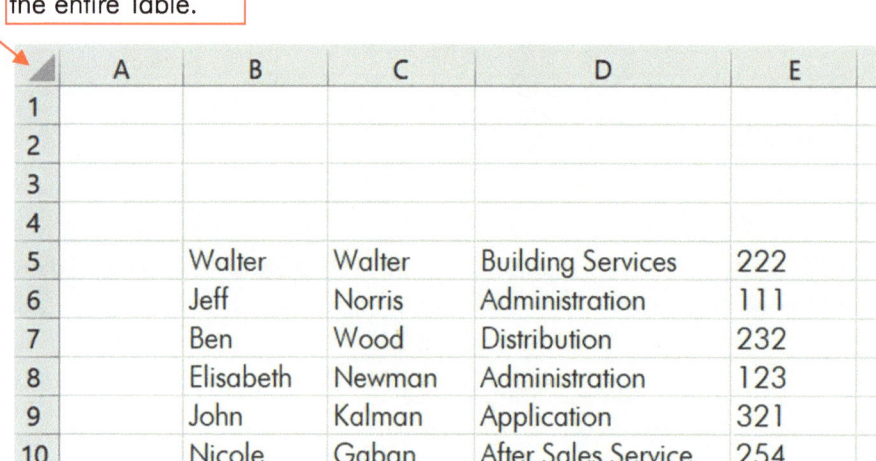

Here you can select the entire Table.

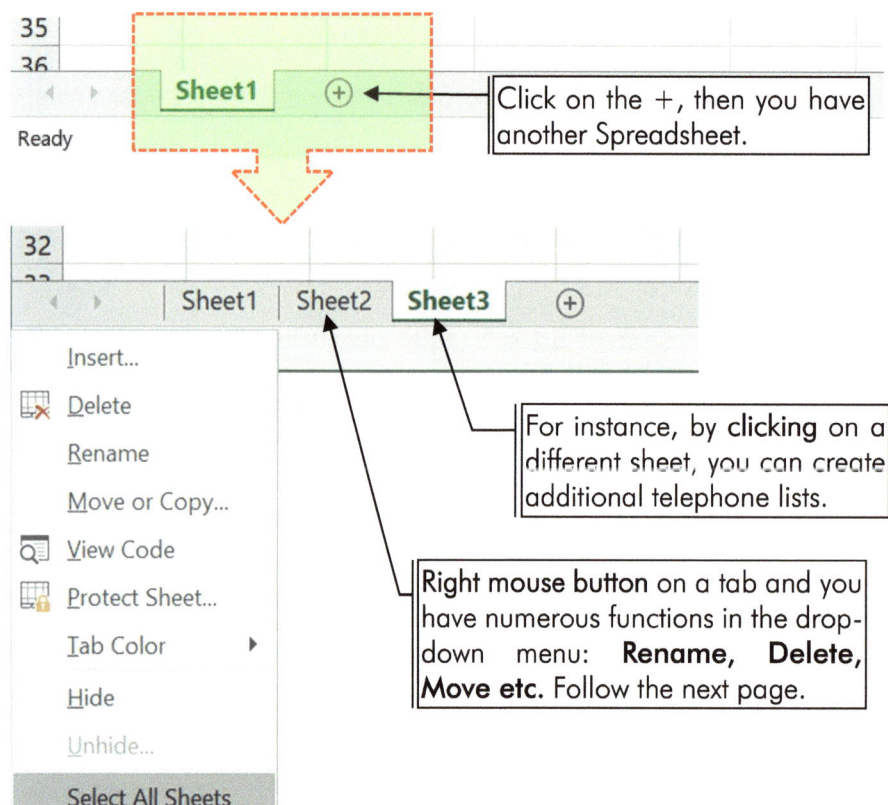

Click on the +, then you have another Spreadsheet.

For instance, by **clicking** on a different sheet, you can create additional telephone lists.

Right mouse button on a tab and you have numerous functions in the drop-down menu: **Rename, Delete, Move etc.** Follow the next page.

➢ Press and hold the left mouse button to **move** the sheets, try this by dragging "Sheet1" between "Sheet2" and "Sheet3".

3.4 Add and Delete Sheets

As empty spreadsheets of this kind do not take up any memory space, they do not disturb, but can be used to extend the current project, such as to create additional Telephone Lists.

This allows you to delete a Sheet:
- Add another **Spreadsheet**.
- Scroll to the new **Spreadsheet**.

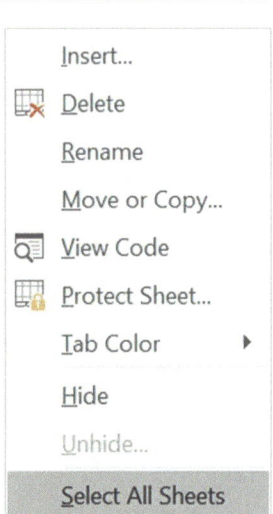

The commands would be in the **Start** menu, but they are much easier to access with the right **mouse button** on a Sheet tab:

- **Insert...** add a new sheet, confirm a standard sheet with Return.

This will add a new spreadsheet, but may not be in the correct position.

Move Sheets:
- Hold the new Spreadsheet (keep the mouse pressed) and **drag** it behind Sheet 2, then release mouse (note arrow).

You can also move several sheets at the same time if you have selected them.

Add several Sheets:
- **Select** Tables 2 and 3 by holding down the [Ctrl] key, you can click and select multiple spreadsheets.
- Then right mouse button at the bottom of the tab and **paste**, then select **spreadsheet** - two new tables have been inserted.

In this way, you could delete several superfluous Sheets:
- **Highlight** sheets 3 to 5 with the mouse (press [Ctrl] key).
- Now **right mouse button** again - select **delete**.

Rename Sheets:
- Either press the **right mouse button** on a tab and choose Rename in the **appearing** menu or
- on the table tab, **double-click** and overwrite,
  - or click again to correct the name specifically.
- Rename the first three spreadsheets to "**House1, 2, 3**":

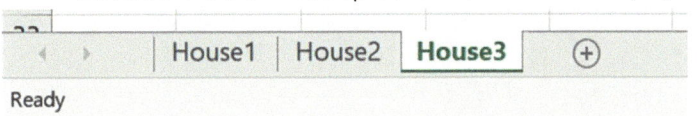

3.5 Rows and Columns

Now we will take a closer look at the table.

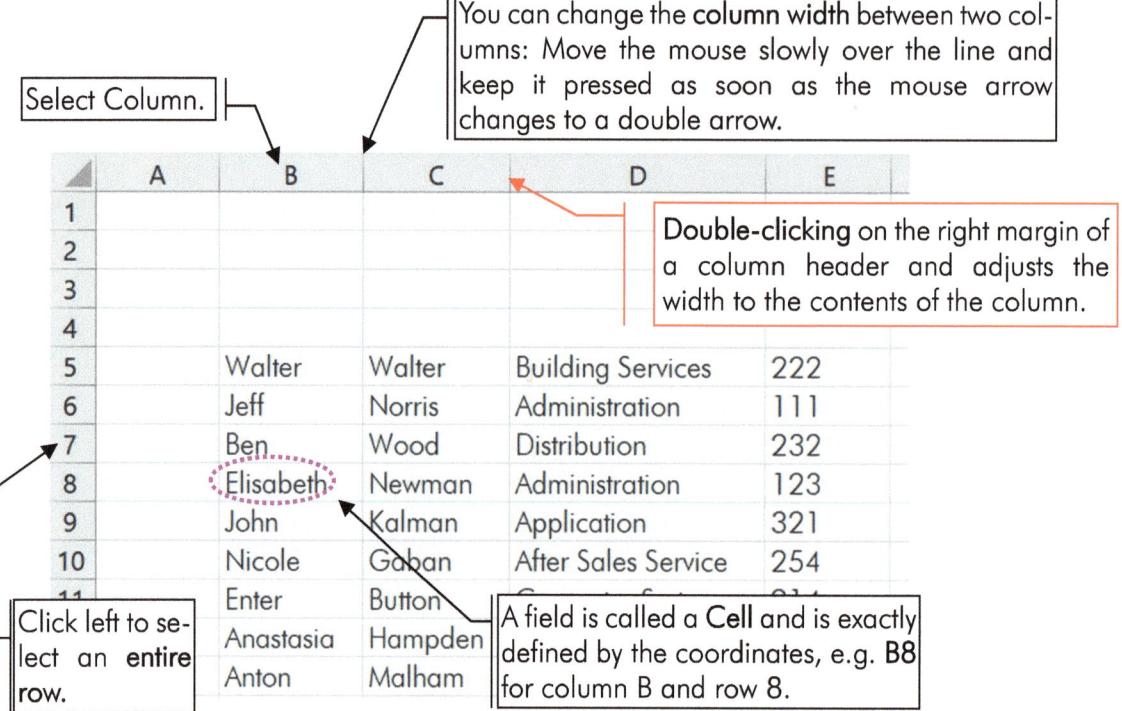

Exercise:

- ➢ **Reduce** the column E with the telephone extension numbers automatically by double-clicking, then manually widen it again slightly.
- ➢ **Widen** column D with the unit.

3.6 The Names of the Columns and Rows

If you look at the previous window, Mr. Fleißig is clearly defined: **column C and line 7** in Excel language C7. These coordinates are important later when entering the formula.

Some Excel purists change the names of the columns so that they are also numbered with numbers. Mr. Fleißig would then be in line 7 and column 3, briefly: **Z7S3**.

The more difficult the calculations become, the more important it is to keep the overview. Because, the numeric column caption was set on some training computers (the default after installation is A B C.... for the columns), here is a note on how you could reset this.

- ➢ This is done at File, then Options and equally
- ➢ for **formulas** - if activated - deactivate reference type **R1C1**.

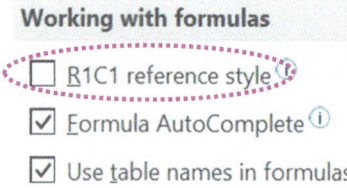

3.7 Copy and Move

- Many actions can be initiated in this way:
  - with the **right mouse button** on the element to be copied or
  - in the Menu with the Icons, for instance for **Cut, Copy, Paste**:

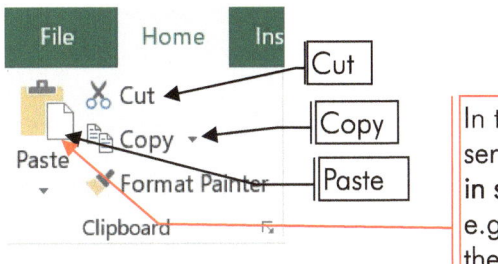

In the drop-down list next to the insert Icon, you will find **insert values in some variations:**
e.g. insert everything, just the value, the formula or the formatting (if a formula has been copied).

The Operating Principle:

- **Cut** copies the selected file to memory and deletes the original, while in the
- **Copy** to keep the Original.
- With both commands, the data copied into the working memory can then be **inserted** as often as required.
  - **Insert** is always at the current cursor position.
  - If something is **selected**, the selected one is replaced when inserting!
- In addition, there are often practical keyboard shortcuts that can be used to copy particularly, quickly, and conveniently:

  - **[Ctrl]-x** for Cut,
  - **[Ctrl]-c** for copying and
  - **[Ctrl]-v** for Insert.

> What is to be copied must be highlighted first.

3.7.1 Copy row

- ➤ **Select** line no. 8 by clicking to the left of it on the line Margin, then press the **Copy** Icon.
- ➤ Now select the next line and **insert** it with **[Ctrl]-v**.

> Note that the existing Data has been overwritten!

- ➤ So **Undo**, then select the next line "John Kalman" and paste **right-click-copied cells**.
  - In this way, the existing line is not overwritten but moved downwards.
- ➤ Change only the first name and extension telephone number for the copy.

3.7.2 Readjusting

Now it's time to make a change. Please note the following:

- First select Rows or Columns, press the right mouse button on the selection, then press **Cut**.
  - This data is memorized in Excel. To prevent data loss, however, it is not Cut until you insert the Data into another location.

- The next stage is **dangerous**, because if you **select** Rows or Columns with existing data,
  - and press Insert, the existing Data will be overwritten, i.e. **deleted**!
  - If this happens unintentionally, **Undo** is the rescue!

> Existing, selected Data is deleted with Insert!

Existing Data is not overwritten with this procedure alone:

- **Select** the Row or Column in front of which the data is to be inserted,
- then press the **right mouse button** on the highlight and select "**Paste cut (or copied) cells**".

Alternatives:

- First insert an empty row by selecting the column in front of which an empty row is to be inserted, then right-click on it and "Paste copied cells".
- To rearrange 3-step technique: first select Cut and Paste somewhere in the empty area, then select, cut and paste at its position, finally Cut the copied path and Paste it to the target position.

Also try this out:

- Move the **column** with the last names to the first position, i.e. before the column with the first names. The procedure described above is also necessary for this purpose.

Chapter 4

4. The Excel Screen

This chapter introduces the Excel interface and draws attention to important areas.

4.1 Quick Access Toolbar and Status Bar

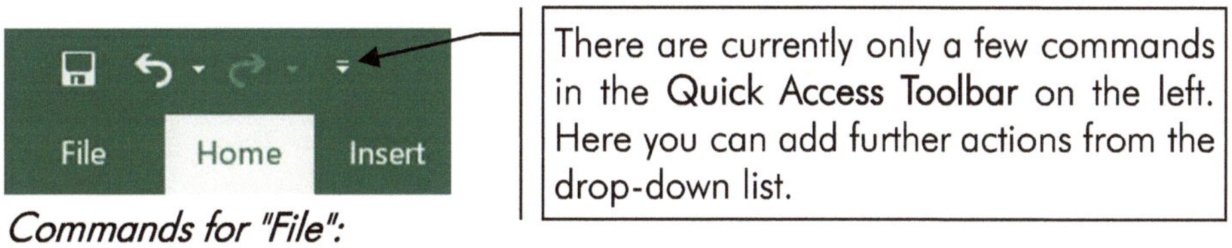
File
Home
Insert
There are currently only a few commands in the Quick Access Toolbar on the left. Here you can add further actions from the drop-down list.

Commands for "File":

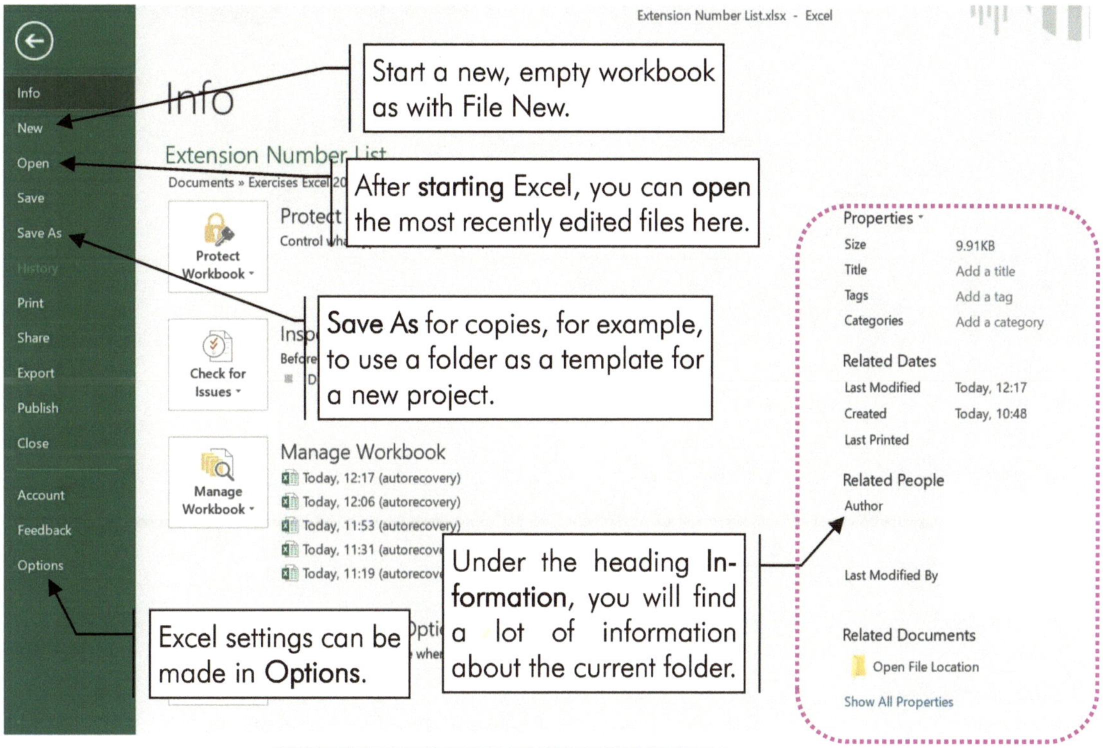
Extension Number List.xlsx - Excel
Info
New
Open
Save
Save As
History
Print
Share
Export
Publish
Close
Account
Feedback
Options
Info
Extension Number List
Protect Workbook
Check for Issues
Manage Workbook
Manage Workbook
Today, 12:17 (autorecovery)
Today, 12:06 (autorecovery)
Today, 11:53 (autorecovery)
Properties
Size
9.91KB
Title
Add a title
Tags
Add a tag
Categories
Add a category
Related Dates
Last Modified
Today, 12:17
Created
Today, 10:48
Last Printed
Related People
Author
Last Modified By
Related Documents
Open File Location
Show All Properties
Start a new, empty workbook as with File New.
After starting Excel, you can open the most recently edited files here.
Save As for copies, for example, to use a folder as a template for a new project.
Under the heading Information, you will find a lot of information about the current folder.
Excel settings can be made in Options.

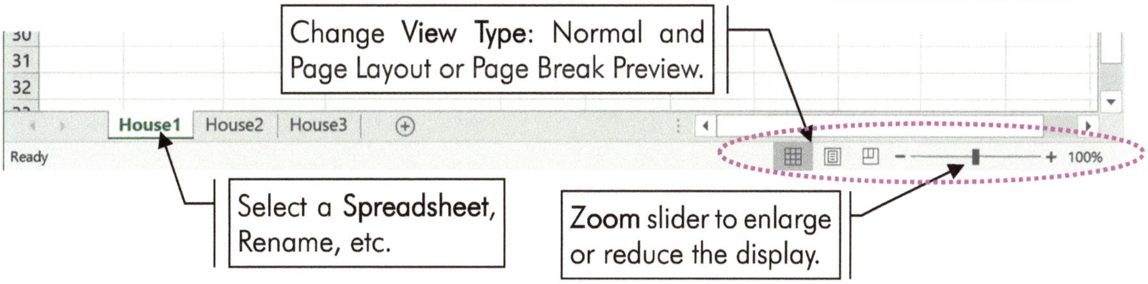
31
32
House1
House2
House3
Ready
100%
Change View Type: Normal and Page Layout or Page Break Preview.
Select a Spreadsheet, Rename, etc.
Zoom slider to enlarge or reduce the display.

4.2 Some important Icons

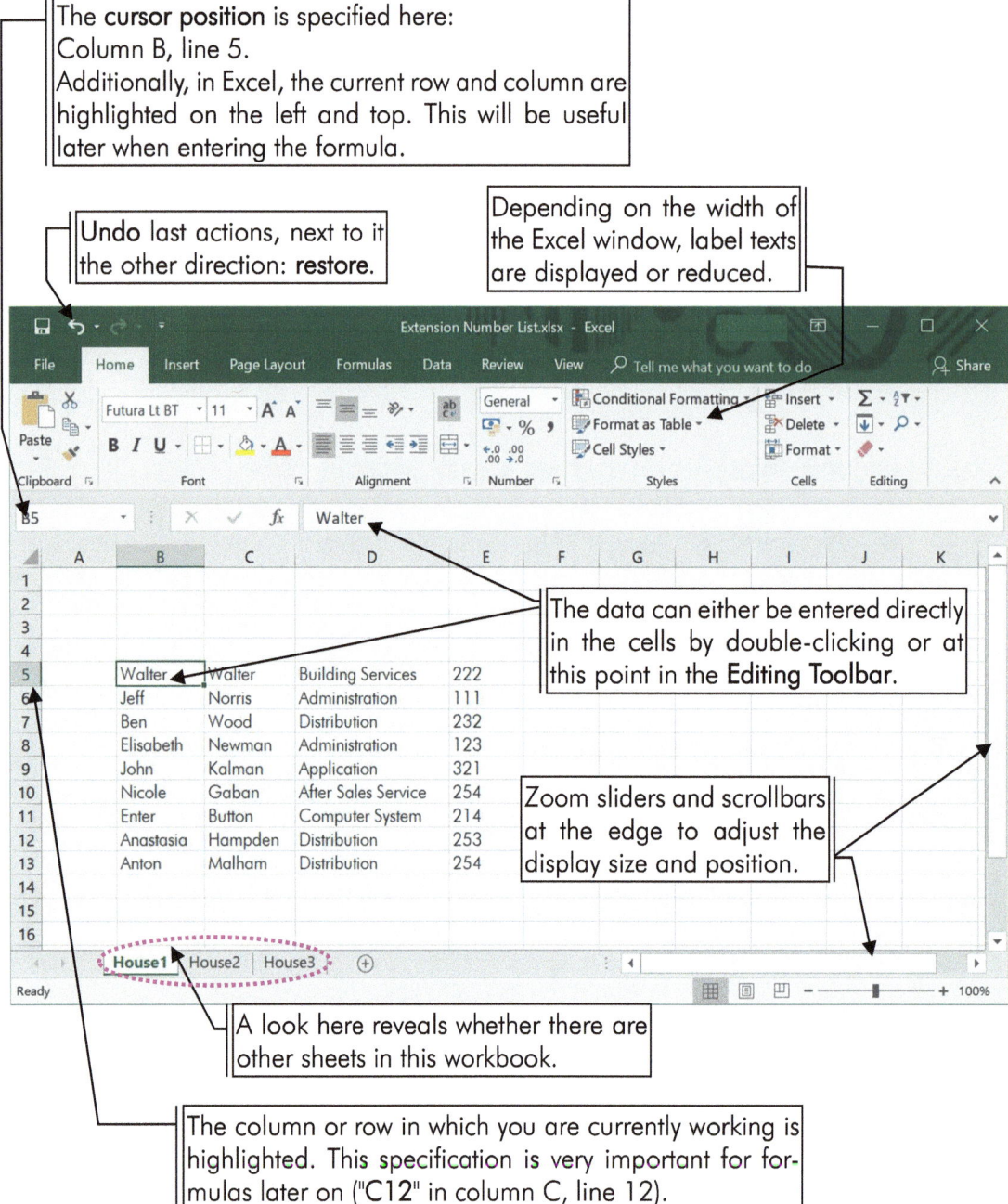

The cursor position is specified here:
Column B, line 5.
Additionally, in Excel, the current row and column are highlighted on the left and top. This will be useful later when entering the formula.

Undo last actions, next to it the other direction: restore.

Depending on the width of the Excel window, label texts are displayed or reduced.

The data can either be entered directly in the cells by double-clicking or at this point in the Editing Toolbar.

Zoom sliders and scrollbars at the edge to adjust the display size and position.

A look here reveals whether there are other sheets in this workbook.

The column or row in which you are currently working is highlighted. This specification is very important for formulas later on ("C12" in column C, line 12).

About the Help:

- If you hold the **mouse** over an icon for a moment, a short description is displayed.
- You [Tell me what you want to do] can enter keywords and search for Return help texts.
- Press [F1] to open the Help menu where you can read the prepared help texts or search for help on a keyword.

4.3 Sort the Columns

After the previous exercise, the column with the last names is in the first position. Use this icon in the Start menu to sort the rows:

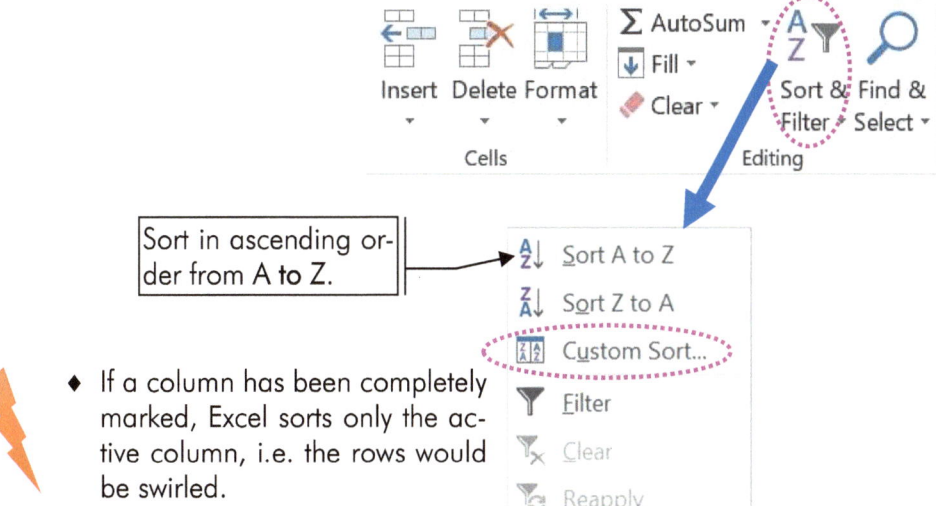

- If a column has been completely marked, Excel sorts only the active column, i.e. the rows would be swirled.

- If only **one column of data** is highlighted, a question "Extend Marking…"

- Only if you extend the selection so that all entries are marked, or if you have marked the entire table right from the start, will be sorted line by line.

  ↪ If necessary, undo immediately, select the entire table and sort it again.

> Check whether you have sorted correctly and completely line by line . You can use the **Undo** and **Redo** icons to check the correct sort or to try the sort function.

➢ Sort by last name, then by **phone number** using "**Custom sorting**", then undo the sorting.

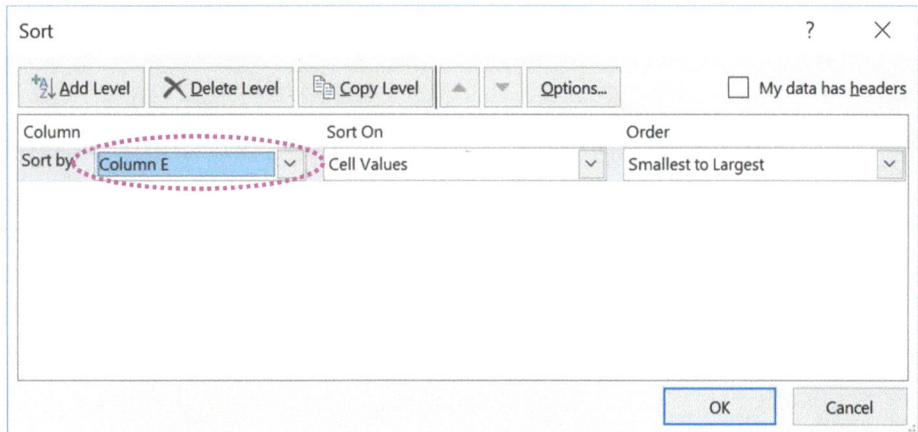

> With "**Custom Sort…**" you can choose which column you want to sort by. If you add a level (icon: Add Level) you can add a second column to sort, too. So you can e.g. first sort the names and if some have same name you can sort second the given names.

4.4 Format-Table

The phone list is now almost ready and should be embellished before Printing. Of course, we can also set everything in Excel: Font, font Size, font Color...

The Icons for formatting are the same on Startup:

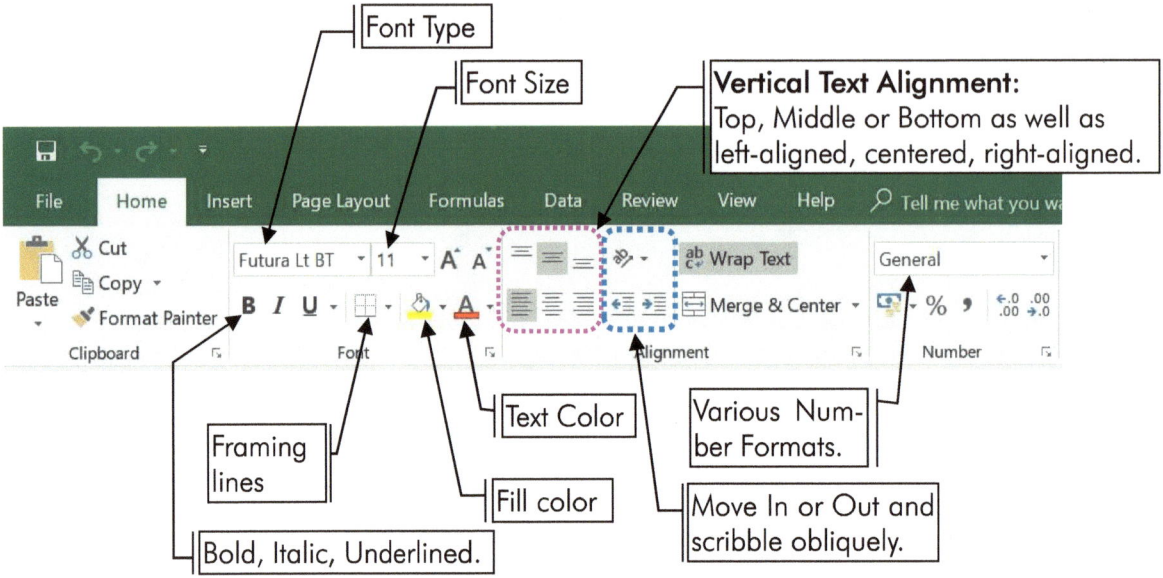

- What is to be changed must be **highlighted** first!
- A **selection list** is expanded when you press the arrow e.g. for Font or Size.

Formatting the Table:

- Format the first column with the **last names**: bold, text color: dark blue, background color: light red.
- Change the font to **Arial**. **Choose Arial** Narrow for the two central columns because it takes up very little space.
- Set the column with the **extension numbers** to bold and dark blue, e.g. with format transfer, **background color** orange.
- Then select all lines and select **frame lines**, for example, all lines first, followed by a thick outer line.

That is how it should be:

Excel is often used to create Tables or Diagrams for **presentations**.
Therefore, we dedicate ourselves in detail to the graphics setting options.

Alternative: try the **cell styles** now (highlight first).

Walter	Walter	Building Services	222
Jeff	Norris	Administration	111
Ben	Wood	Distribution	232
Elisabeth	Newman	Administration	123
John	Kalman	Application	321
Nicole	Gaban	After Sales Service	254
Enter	Button	Computer System	214
Anastasia	Hampden	Distribution	253
Anton	Malham	Distribution	254

4.5 The Page View

Before each **Printout**, the current table should be checked again in the Page Layout view. Not only for checking, but also because the document can be excellently formatted there.

➤ Switch to **Page Layout** instead of Normal on the page layout tab:

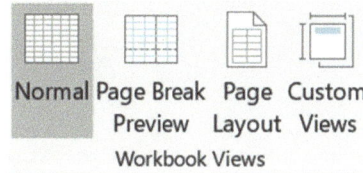

Here you can see how the table would be Printed:

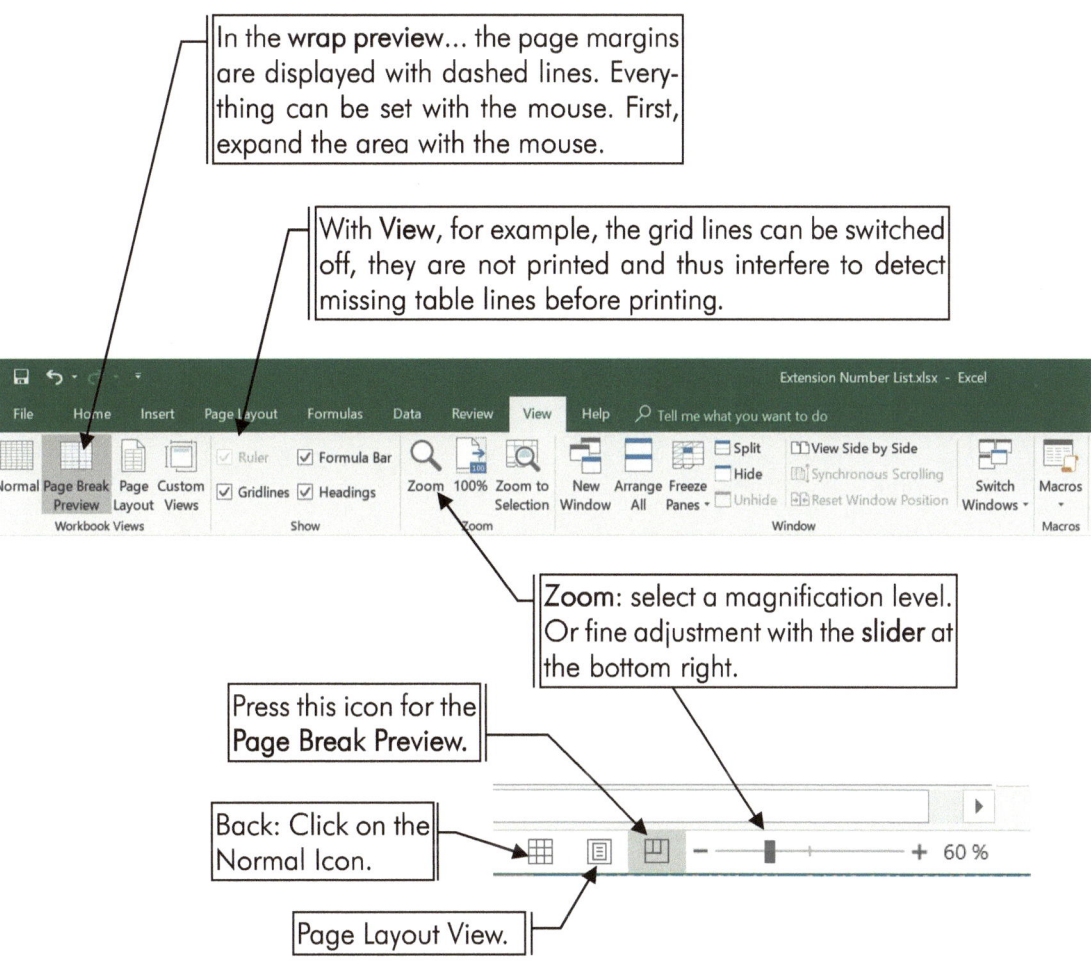

In the **wrap preview**... the page margins are displayed with dashed lines. Everything can be set with the mouse. First, expand the area with the mouse.

With **View**, for example, the grid lines can be switched off, they are not printed and thus interfere to detect missing table lines before printing.

Zoom: select a magnification level. Or fine adjustment with the **slider** at the bottom right.

Press this icon for the **Page Break Preview**.

Back: Click on the Normal Icon.

Page Layout View.

➤ **Try** it out: Zoom with the Icon and lower right with the Slider, use the mouse to move borders in the page break preview, switch off the display of gridlines.

♦ In the **break preview,** you can define which position a new page is to start if the table does not fit on one sheet.

   ↪ Existing page breaks (thick lines) can be moved with the **left mouse button,**

   ↪ with "**Insert right mouse button page break**" you can set a **page change** at the current cursor position.

From the **View** menu, you can select the view type or switch to another Workbook.

4.6 Page Setup

The menu for setting up the page (paper size, margins...) can be found on the **Page Layout** tab.

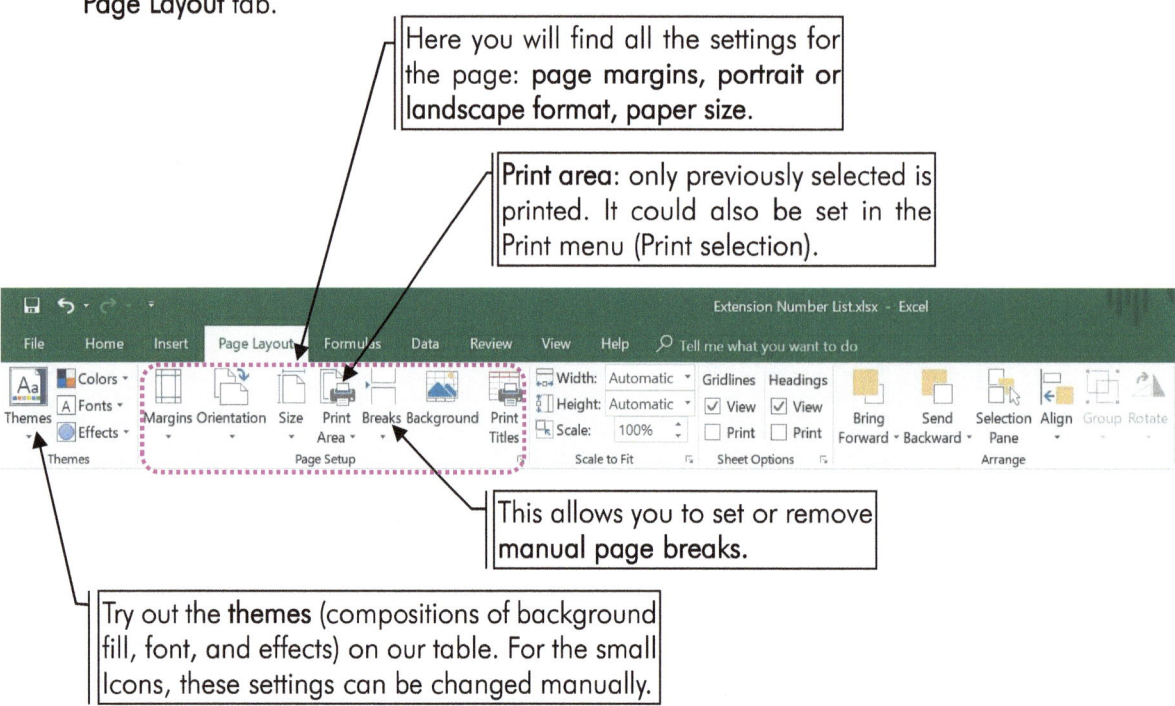

Here you will find all the settings for the page: **page margins, portrait or landscape format, paper size.**

Print area: only previously selected is printed. It could also be set in the Print menu (Print selection).

This allows you to set or remove **manual page breaks**.

Try out the **themes** (compositions of background fill, font, and effects) on our table. For the small Icons, these settings can be changed manually.

Choose the Break Preview:

> To practice the presentation and settings for several pages, copy the address list and paste it into the **page break** preview until we have more than one page of data without long paperwork.

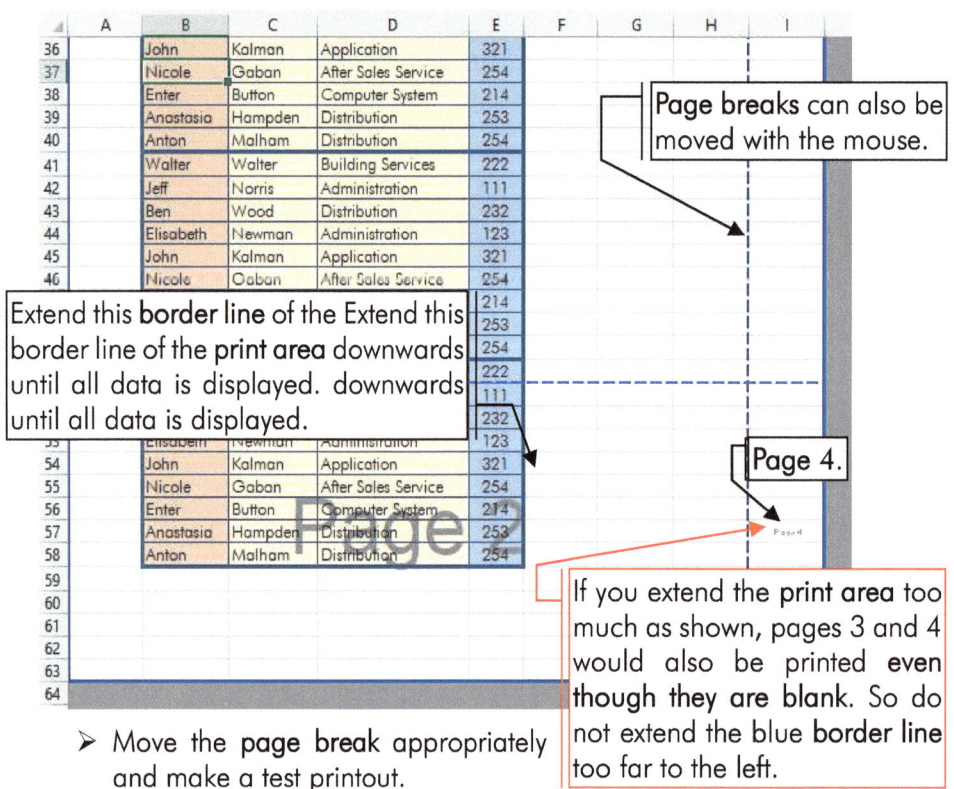

Page breaks can also be moved with the mouse.

Extend this **border line** of the Extend this border line of the **print area** downwards until all data is displayed. downwards until all data is displayed.

Page 4.

If you extend the **print area** too much as shown, pages 3 and 4 would also be printed **even though they are blank**. So do not extend the blue **border line** too far to the left.

> Move the **page break** appropriately and make a test printout.

4.7 Header and Footer, Page Setup

Go to the Page Layout tab:

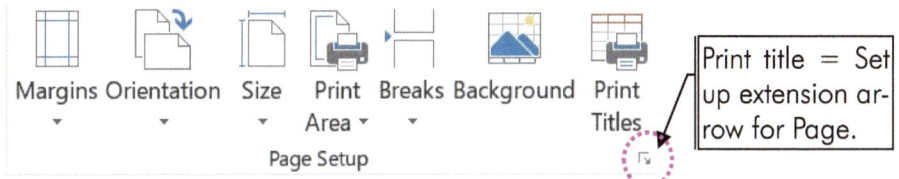

*The **Print Titles button** opens the same menu as Page Setup:*

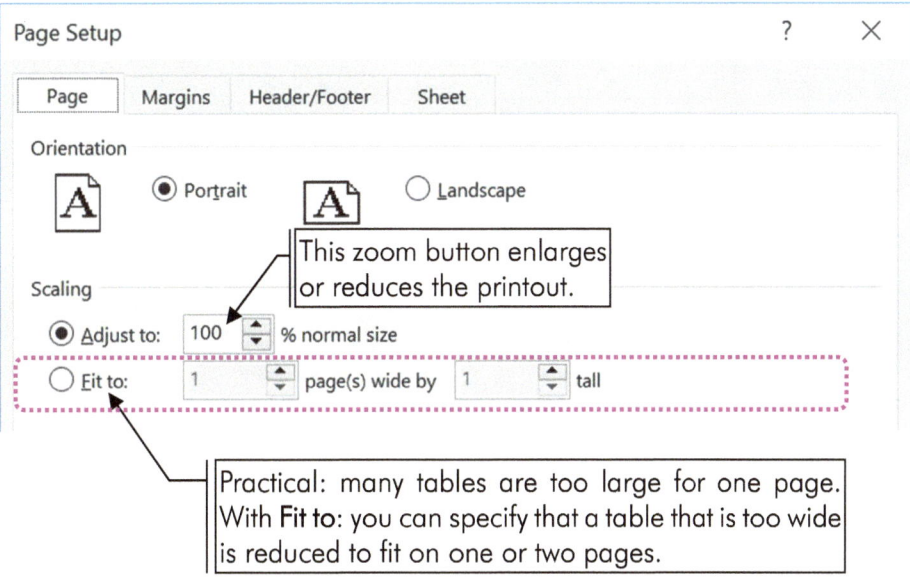

More about the Page Setup menu = Print Title:

- **Page Margin tabs**: sometimes it is useful to have a table **centered horizontally or vertically** for printing.
- **Header/Footer** tab: the **data** of the Excel tables are saved in the middle section above which you can set up a Header, below which a Footer can be retrieved on each page.
  - ↳ *Practical* e.g. for the name of the table, page number, date etc.
  - ↳ The size of the header or footer can be entered in the **margins tab**:

4.7.1 Set up Header and Footer

We can customize the header according to our preferences, switch in above menu to "**Header/Footer**". This can be done in two ways:

- The simplest one: select a preset from the drop-down list.
  - ↳ Here you can select an Entry, e.g. "**Page 1 of** ?" or the table name, which will then be centered.

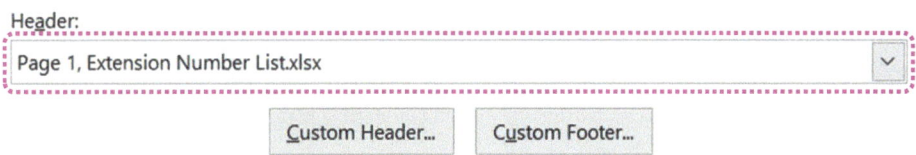

If several entries are to be placed in a Header or Footer, you can select the "**C**ustom Header" or "**C**ustom Footer" **button.**

- This allows various entries to be arranged either on the left, centered or in the right area of the header or footer:

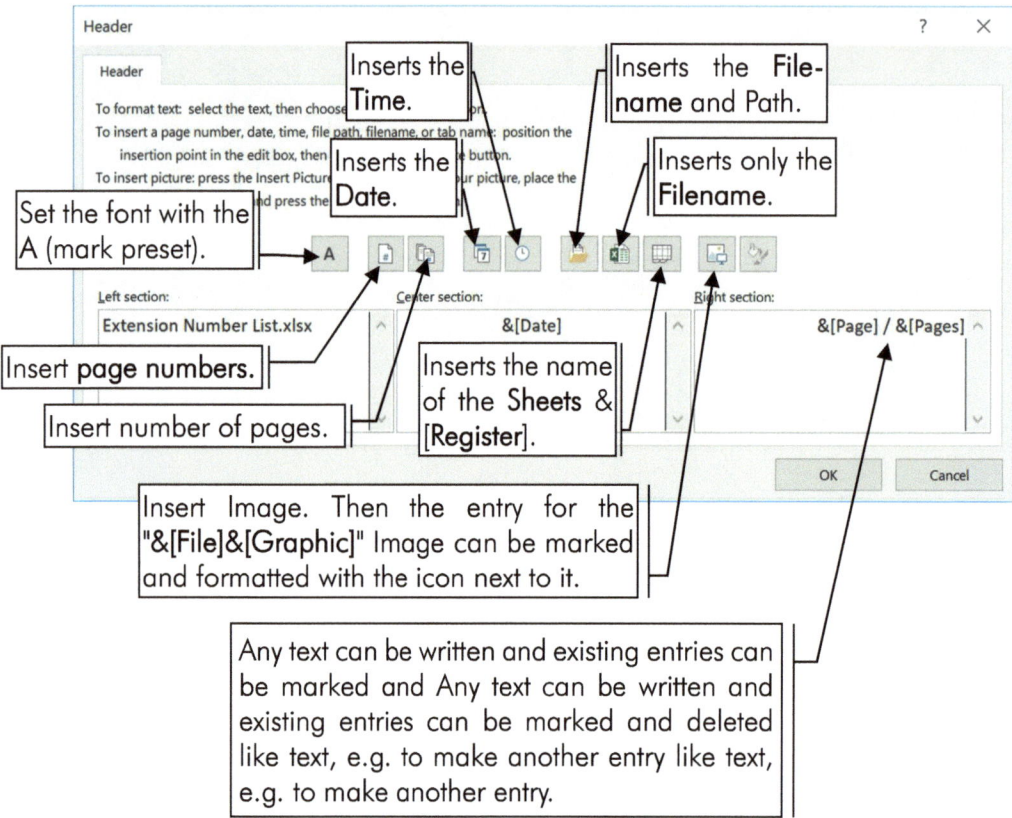

- Enter the **filename** as shown on the left **with date and location** in the middle: for example, type **Munich**, then insert the date behind it.
- On the right is the current page number & number of pages, e.g.: page &[page] of &[pages] pages.
  - Write **Page**, then press the Icon for **Pages** behind it,
  - then **from** Type and Insert the Icon for the **number of pages**, the printout will be displayed, that is **Page 2 of 6 pages**.
- Format all components with **9 dots font size**.

Additional View and some helpful Shortcuts:

- Header or Footer can also be edited directly in the **Page Layout** view.
  - **[Ctrl]-a** selects the entire Table,
  - **[Ctrl]-[End]** and you are at the end of the Table,
  - **[Ctrl]-[Pos 1]** takes you to the beginning,
  - **[Ctrl]-[Shift]-[End]** selected from the current cursor position to the end of the sheet, - [Pos 1] to the beginning.

Shortcuts

4.8 Convert to Table

This Table can be converted into a real Table, which was previously only loose data for Excel. This means that Excel knows that the rows belong to each other and must be arranged together when Sorting, or that formatting must belong for the entire Table.

> This function allows normal table editing for managing data records (not for calculation) in Excel.

- Select Table on the **Insert tab page**.
- Usually, Excel detects the Table when you click on it, please note the **dashed selection frame**, otherwise, select the table by holding down the mouse button.

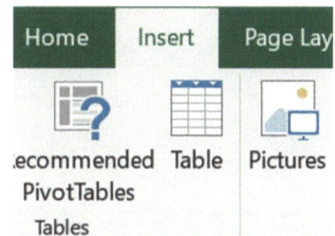

- We have no Headers, so do not select: "Table has Headers". Excel automatically inserts Headers, which should then be renamed accordingly.

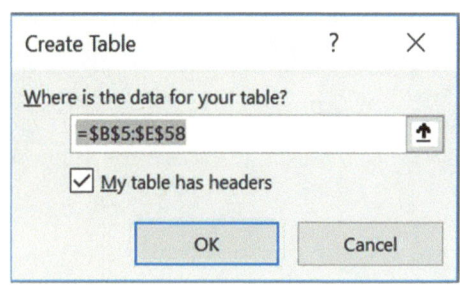

You then have the **column tabs** with which you can sort the table or apply certain filters for file selection.

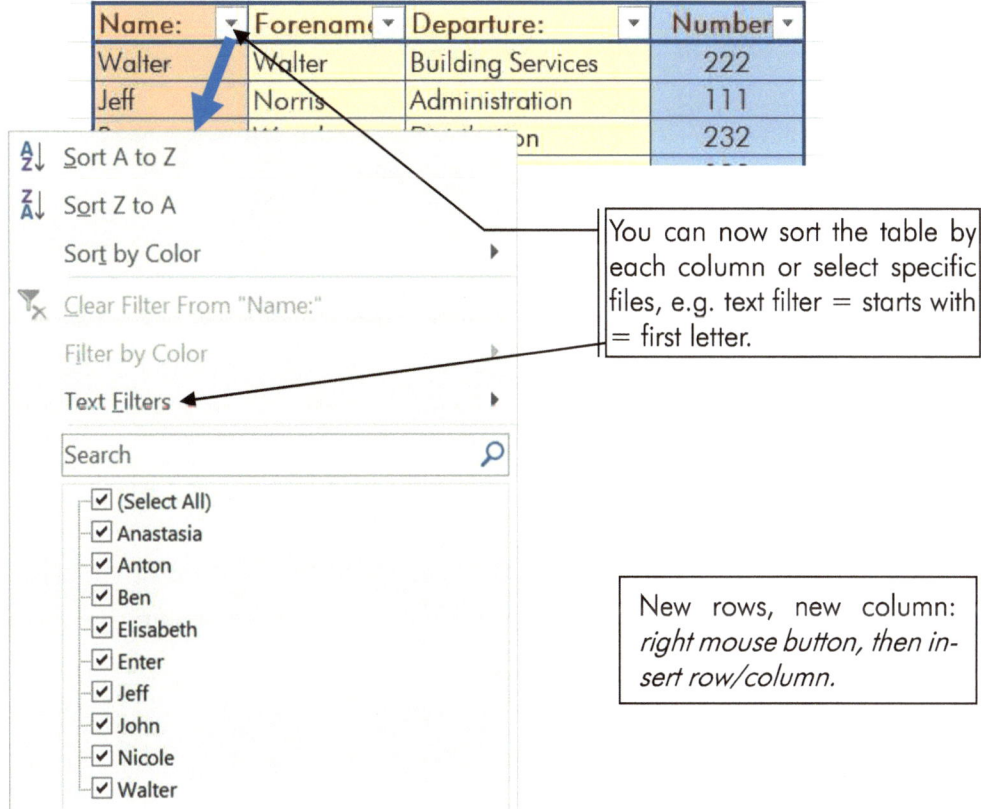

You can now sort the table by each column or select specific files, e.g. text filter = starts with = first letter.

New rows, new column: *right mouse button, then insert row/column.*

4.9 Summary

This was a little excursus on formatting, from which you should have taken the following:

General Information:

- You must first change the text before you can change the **font**.
  _____

- In a **database**, the emphasis is on compiling of
  _____

- For a **spreadsheet** on the execution of
  _____

Sorting and copying:

- Where to find the Icon for **Sorting**: _____
- What has to be considered when **Sorting**? _____
- What are the three shortcuts for **Cut, Copy, Paste** that apply to each program? _____
- Also create the **Icons** for the commands above: _____

Setting and Formatting:

- How do you get to the menu to set the **Page margins**? There are two ways to do this:
  _____
  _____
  _____

- What is the characteristic of a **Header or Footer**?
  _____

The Scroll Bar:

- What is the fastest way to get to the middle of a long table using the Scrollbar?
  _____

- How do you see your current position in a spreadsheet in the Scrollbar?
  _____

- Which shortcut key takes you to the **beginning** of a Table?
  _____

Part 2

CALCULATIONS IN EXCEL

Sum and other Formulas, copy formulas relative or absolute, the Formula editor

5. Calculate a Sum

Now we come step by step to the main applications of Excel to perform various calculations.

- ♦ This helps, for instance, with:
  - ↳ Calculations,
  - ↳ Architects can determine the size of apartments,
  - ↳ all calculations: Building loan agreement, Leasing or Purchase, Real estate financing, statistical Evaluations, test Evaluations,
  - ↳ Calculate Income and Expenses, etc.
- ♦ The big advantage is that the calculations, once set up,
  - ↳ are **automatically** executed and updated.
  - ↳ This allows you to experiment with different values, such as down payments of 5,000, 8,000 or 10,000 for car leasing.

5.1 Preparation of the Exercise

Formula is inserted for Excel to calculate.

- ➤ Start a **new Workbook** and save it (in our folder!) under the name **Total Sales per Region**.
- ➤ **Create** the following Table:

Total Sales per Region	
Region 1	34.555
Region 2	4.536
Region 3	34.345
Region 4	75.567
Region 5	104.223
Sum:	
All Values in Euro	

The formula is inserted into this cell to calculate the total automatically.
You could click on the cell "=" and enter the Formula b2+b3+b4+b5+b6.
"The second line in column b is "b2".
The next page presents more convenient input options.

LINDEMANN GROUP © MSc (UAS) PETER SCHIESSL   37

5.2 The Input Options

There are numerous ways to enter Formulas.

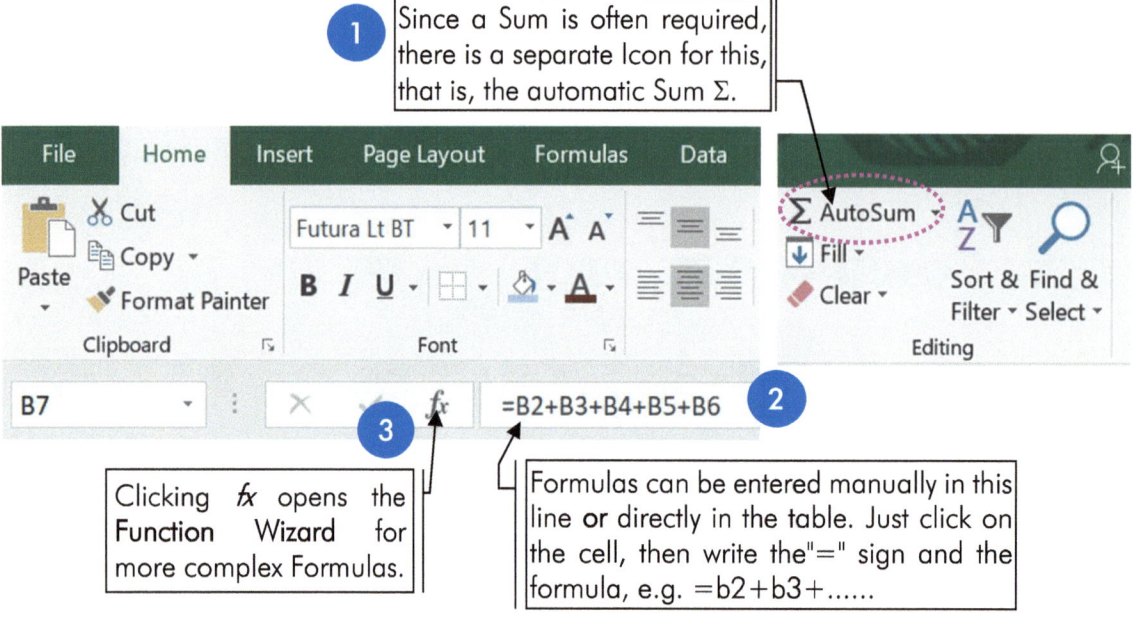

5.3 The automatic Sum

Try the following variants for the Sum:

- First, click on the Cell in which the Sum is to be inserted.
- Press the Icon for the automatic **Sum**, then press Return.

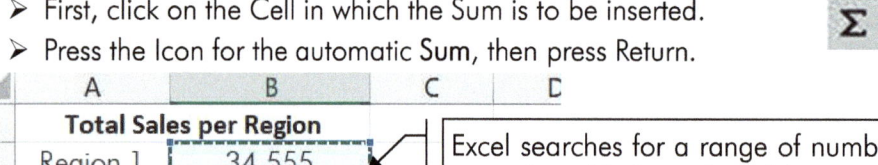

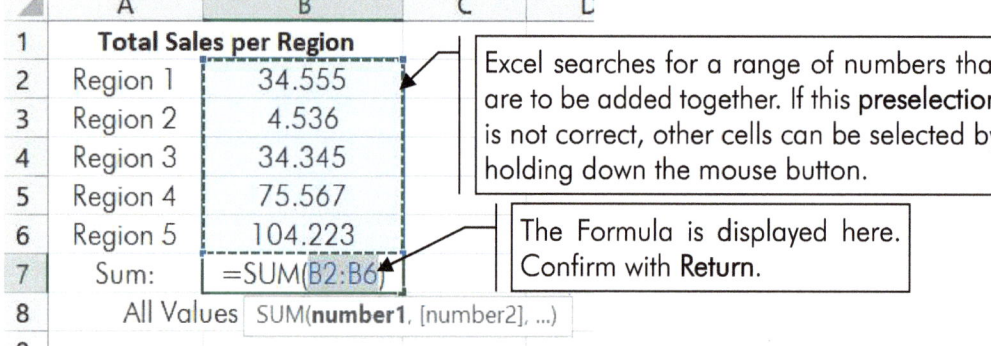

- ♦ The Entry = Sum (B2: B6) is easy to understand if you remember that each cell is determined by the coordinates:
  - ↳ Add Data in the second **column B** and in **rows 2 to 6**.
  - ↳ The entry: =**Sum** (**B2:B6**) corresponds to this longer Entry: =B2+B3+B4+B5+B6. The + signs would **not** require a "Sum" formula.

Complete the Exercise:

- Finally, confirm the formula with **Return**.
- **Change** the value in Region 2 from 4,536 to 44,536 and watch the Sum update automatically after **Return**.

5.4 Complete the Table

Formatting is quickest with these Icons:

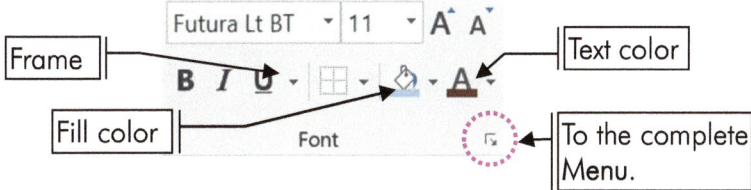

Procedure:

- **Select** Line, then at
  - an Icon, e.g. fill color, press the **arrow** (▼) and
  - in the **options menu** to select a different color.

With the **extension arrow** or with the **right mouse button format Cells** you can access a dialog window with all setting options:

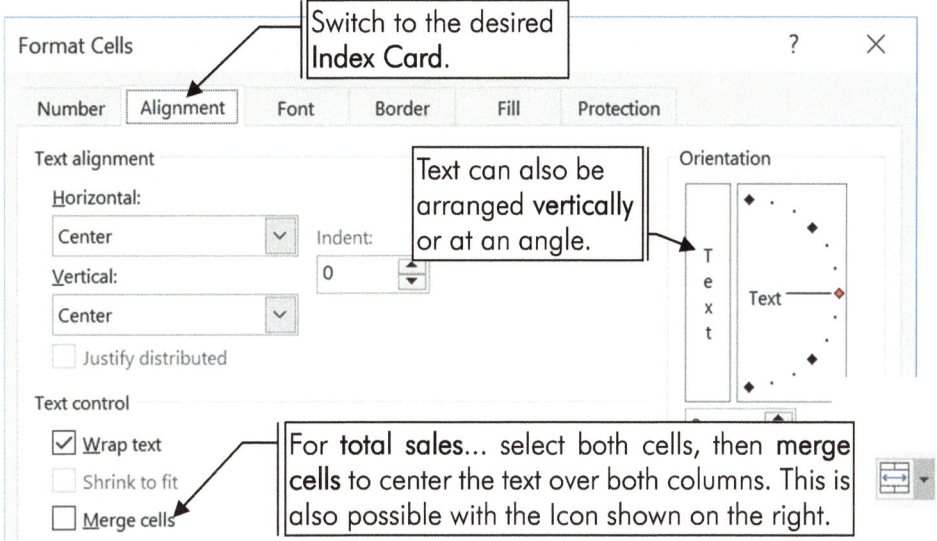

As a Suggestion:
Exercises for the Calculations
Table 1   Status: (Date)

In the **Header**.

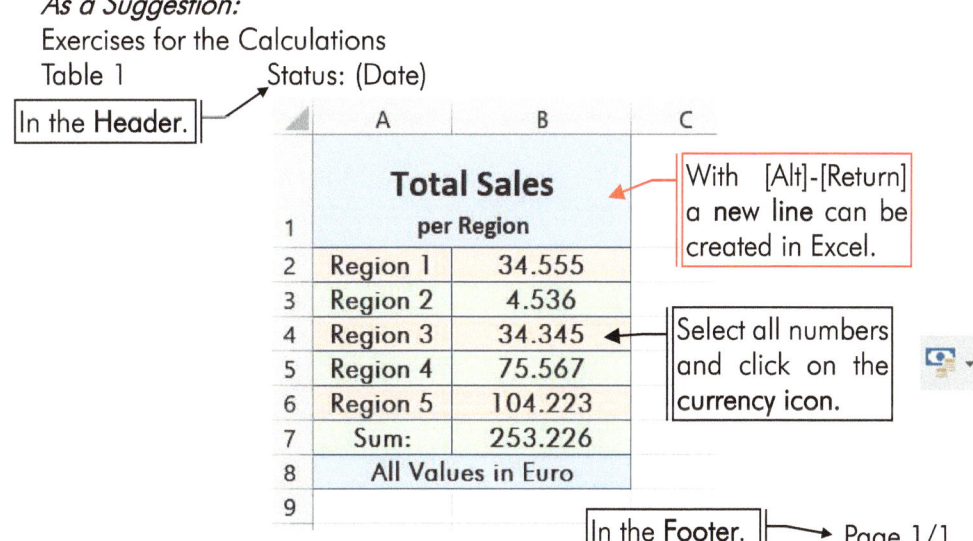

With [Alt]-[Return] a **new line** can be created in Excel.

Select all numbers and click on the currency icon.

In the **Footer**. → Page 1/1

- ➢ **Format** the Table: Font, Position, Fill Color, etc. until it looks nice and **prints** the table after a review in the Page Layout and Preview page.

5.5 New Month, New Sheet, Rename

As we have enough sheets, we don't need to overwrite this table or start a new workbook for next month.

- ➢ Add three **more spreadsheets**: Press Icon or right mouse button on a tab, then insert.

- ➢ **Select** all values in the Table while holding down the mouse button.
- ➢ **Press** Copy (Icon),
- ➢ to switch to the second spreadsheet and **paste** the copied table there, then also to the third and fourth sheets and also paste.
- ➢ In the copied new tables, insert **different values** and rename the worksheets after the month.

To make it perfect, we rename the Sheets:

Table 1 becomes Jan18,
Table 2 to February 18,
etc.

Renaming

- ♦ These practical **options** are available for **Renaming**:
  - ↳ **right mouse button** on the sheet tab, then **rename** or
  - ↳ **double-click** the sheet tab, then **overwrite** the text or click again and correct.
- ➢ **Rename** the Sheets as shown.

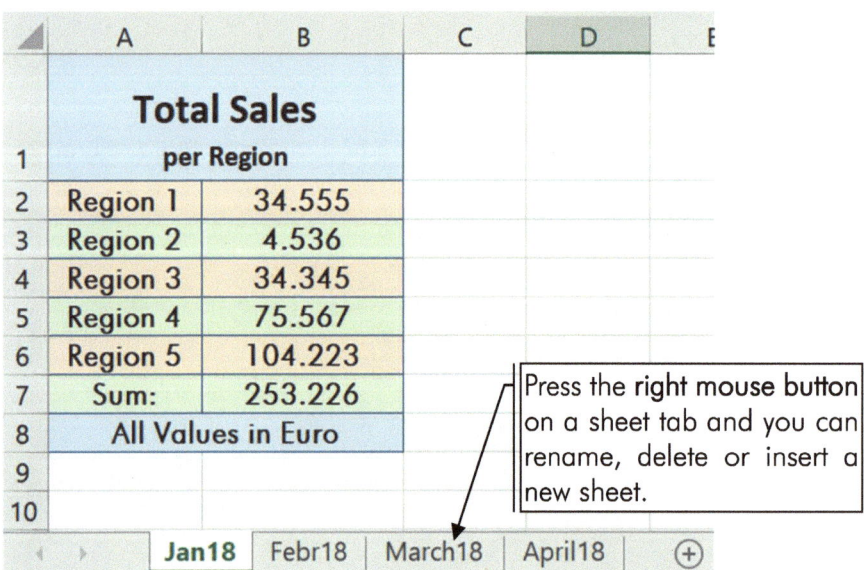

6. Formula and Coordinates

The square footage of an apartment is to be determined.

> Start all over: start a new **folder** and save it as an **apartment calculation**.
> Create the following table on **Sheet 1**:

Start in cell **B3**. You don't have to start at the top left. It often makes more sense to leave a few lines blank so that Headers can be added later.

After entering the values, double-click between the column tabs to **automatically** adjust the column width.

Merge the cells of the Heading, followed by formatting.

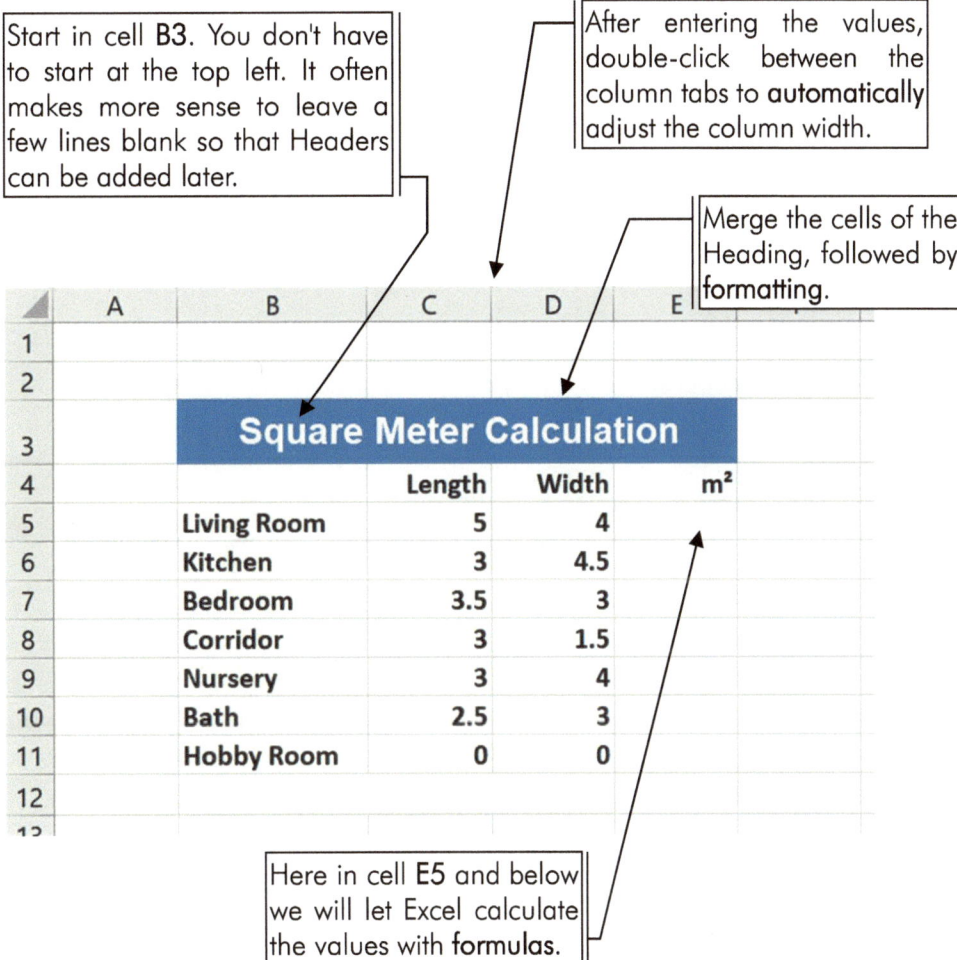

Here in cell **E5** and below we will let Excel calculate the values with **formulas**.

There are several ways to enter the formula. First, we will give the formula with the easiest and most practical method suitable for such simple calculations: by **pointing** with the mouse.

6.1 Quick Entry by Pointing

The formula is specified only once, followed by multiple copies to the bottom.

Enter formula with Pointer:

- Click E5 to select this cell,
- then = type and click with the mouse on the cell C5 with the value 5,
- * (for multiplication) type, then
- click on the next value 4 to be multiplied in cell D5.   *pointing*
- The formula is ready and can be completed with **Return**.

About "Pointing":

- Abled by **Pointing**
  - click on **each cell** one after the other to add remote values,
  - as well as several contiguous cells with a **Frame**.

If the **Excel suggestion** does not fit in a formula, the correct cells can be specified in this way.

This shows you the input with the **sum-icon** and the most practical method by **pointing** with the mouse, which is now used in some exercises until the **formula-wizard** is required for more complicated formulas.   *Σ ▾*

6.2 Copy Formula

We do not need to re-enter this formula in each cell.

- Click on the cell with the Formula,
- then **Copy** formula: fastest with **[Ctrl]-C** (C for Copy),   *[Ctrl]-C*
- then select all of the following cells with the left mouse button pressed and choose   *[Ctrl]-V*
- **insert** the Formula: with the Icon or the Shortcut **[Ctrl]-V**.

> Note that the references in the new, copied formulas have been changed automatically, for example, C6*D6 is calculated instead of C5*D5, **then** C7*D7 and so on. Click on the following cells for more information.

We have just copied the formula **relatively** because Excel has adjusted the values to be multiplied relative to the position of **the formula**.   *relative*

6.3 Insert the result with Sum

We need a Sum of Fields E5 to E11.

> You can do this with the Sum-Icon:

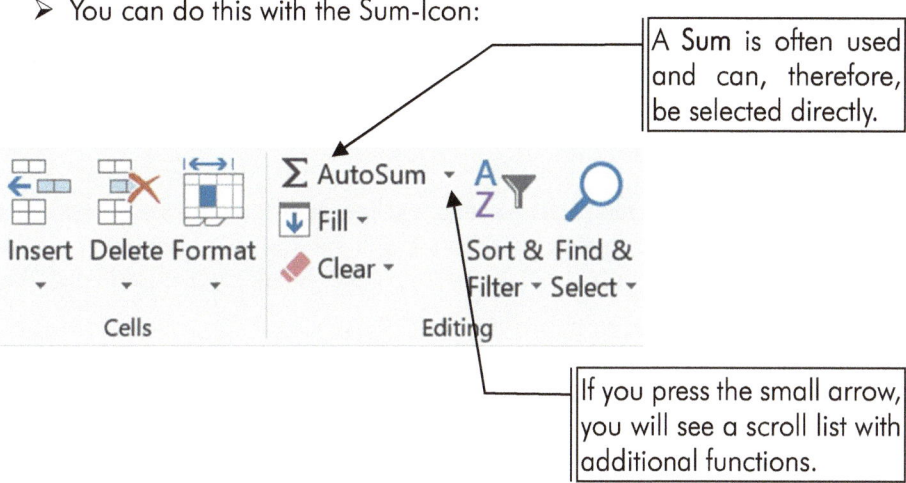

A Sum is often used and can, therefore, be selected directly.

If you press the small arrow, you will see a scroll list with additional functions.

> Click on the calculated Sum and look at the formula at the top of the **formula line**, which Excel has automatically inserted.

♦ Consequently, the expression (E5: E11) stands for the fields from E5 to E11, from which, depending on the formula, for example

- Sum(E5:E11) = E5+E6+…+E10+E11 or
- Product(E5:E11) = E5*E6*…*E10*E11.

6.4 Absolute and Relative Coordinates

This is the right place for some theoretical remarks about the Excel language.

6.4.1 Relative References

Normally, as we have just done, we work with relative coordinates. An example:

	A	B	C
1	55	556	
2	234	334	
3	=A1+A2	=B1+B2	

Relative references, therefore, mean: the coordinates are adjusted relative to the position when moving or copying.

If you copy this formula =A1+A2 into the next column, Excel automatically enters: =B1+B2 so that we can easily copy formulas into other cells.

6.4.2 Absolute References

If you want to copy the formula absolutely unchanged in exceptional cases, such as when a result is to be used elsewhere.

Excel does **not** automatically adjust the references if a **$ character** (dollar) precedes a coordinate specification. In the example above, the formula would be:

=$A$1+$A$2

- Note that one $ character is required for each column **and** row. This makes it possible, for example, to set only the column absolute, but still leave the row changeable (relative) or vice versa: the column absolute $A1 only, the row absolute A$1 only.

You can copy this formula"=$A$1+$A$2" into any cell. The value entered for A1 and A2 is always added, even if you change the values in these cells. Thus you can use this result in other places including other sheets.

6.4.3 Copy Formula Absolute

If you want to copy formulas without this automatic update, then proceed as follows:

- Either precede values that are not to be changed (=they are to be absolute) with a $ or
- click on the cell, select the formula in the **editing line** and **copy** it there, but then cancel with [Esc] so that this line remains unchanged.

- Now you have the formula with **absolute reference** in the working memory and can insert it into any number of other cells, but only on the **current sheet**.
- Type below the table: "The apartment has a total of:", this right-aligned, then insert the formula in the next cell and "square meters" in the following cell.

6.4.4 Replacements

Also, if you want to add a long list, you do not have to specify all cells. You can (see the previous example) select the cells to be added with the mouse or enter the coordinates directly. The Colon specifies ranges.

A small selection:

A5:C20   The area between column A, row 5 and column C, row 20.

5:20   All cells between row 5 and row 20.

B: B   All cells in column B.

- Try this: set the formula Sum(D: D) in any cell.

6.5 Creating the Headline

First, the Headline. This should be inverted for a change (white letters on dark background):

Square Meter Calculation

- ➢ Select Dark Blue with the **fill color** and **Yellow** with the icons.

- ➢ In addition, set a larger font, approx. **16 points**, to connect all four columns.

Row Height and Column Width:

- ♦ Manual: click on a row with the right mouse button on the left margin, this highlights it and the drop-down menu appears, in which you can enter the **row height** for row height, as well as for a column if a column was selected at the top of the column tabs.

- ♦ You can widen the **edges** of the columns and row tabs with the mouse or have them automatically adjusted to the content by double-clicking.

- ♦ Automatic: when **starting**, you will find the command Adjust **row height automatically** in the **drop-down** list under **Format**, as well as for the column height.

  - ✎ If the font is larger, a **larger line height** is automatically set. In case the font is **cut off**, select this function or increase the row height.

Commands for formatting cells can be found under Home Format:

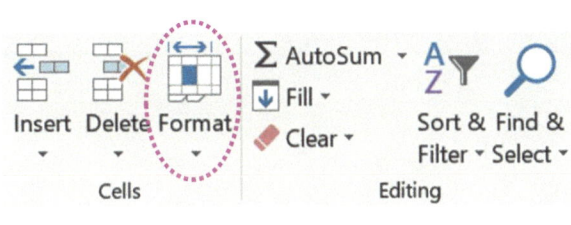
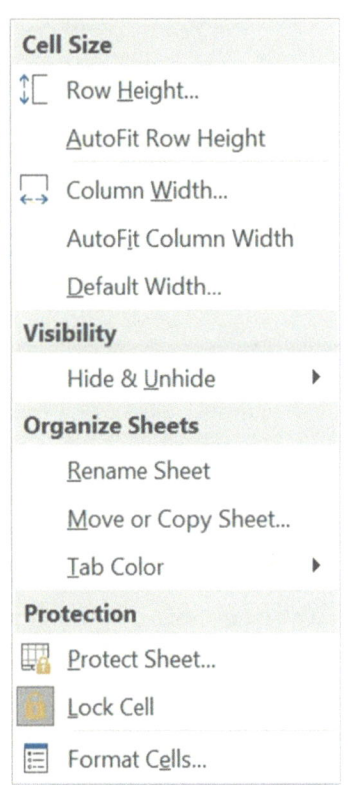

6.6 Transfer Format

This time, we will format the rest of the table in a different and faster way. We will not re-set each line, but only one and its settings will be transferred to the other lines with a command provided for this purpose.

This allows us to set tables much faster in which the lines are in **two colors** for a better Overview.

This is how it's supposed to be:

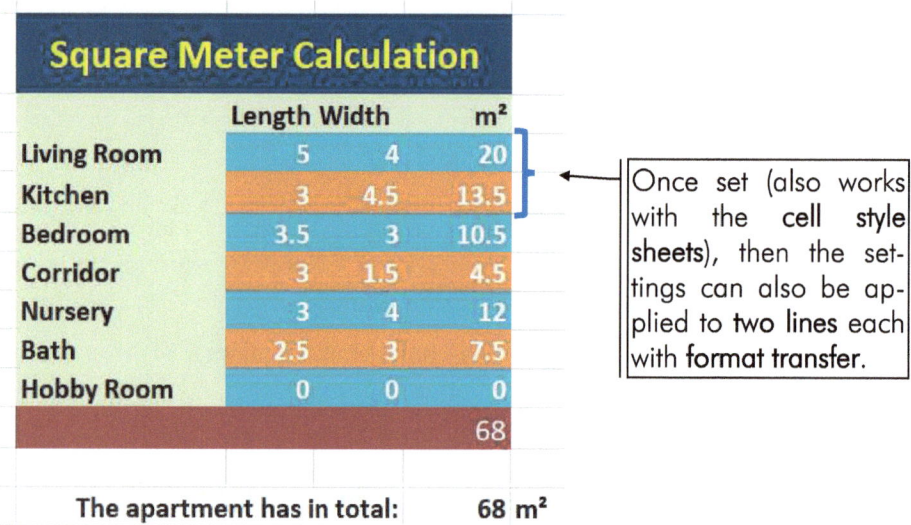

- ➢ **Select** the numbers 5, 4 and 20 for Living room.
  - ➢ Use the **fill icon** or the **cell styles** to set the **background color** to light blue, then also for the second row with a lighter background.

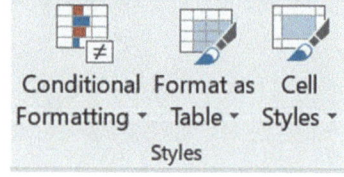

- ➢ Select both rows (only cells with a colored background) and double-click the **Transfer Format** icon:
- ➢ Now the other lines can be highlighted and formatted in the same way.
- ➢ Finally, click on **Transfer format** again to **deactivate** this function.

Click or double-click on format transfer?

- ♦ Double-click **Transfer format** to activate it and remain active until this function is deactivated by pressing it again.
- ♦ If you click **Transfer format** only once, the formatting can be copied only once.

Complete the Exercise:

- The **entire** table is highlighted in red and in bold while the **row** and **column titles** are in blue, which means the table is ready.
- Adjust the **page preview** in the center, adjust the Header and Footer and **print** the entire calculation.

> It is possible to transfer two lines of different colors to the next two lines at once. Very practical for spreadsheets.

6.7 Room Calculation Exercise

To practice the formula entry a bit more, we will calculate some more sums.

- Excel **suggests** the numbers on the left (empty above) or above for formulas.
- If other values are to be included in the calculation, this is very simply possible by clicking with the mouse (**point**).

Create the following Exercise:

	Square Meter		
	House 1	*House 2*	*House 3*
R1	55	90	33
R2	55	67	100
R3	90	40	33
R4	67		
Sum:	**267**	**197**	**166**
Total:	**630** (House 1 + House 2 + House 3)		

Enter formula with Display: **Display**

- Click the cell next to **Total**,
- then = type and click with the mouse 267,
- type +, then,
- click to add the next value 197,
- again, click + and 166,
- the formula is ready and can be completed with **Return**.

If the **Excel suggestion** does not fit in a formula, the correct cells can be specified in this way.

Chapter 7

7. The Function Wizard

Now we will look at the function wizard which can be used to enter more complex formulas. Simple formulas by pointing, while more difficult formulas are selected from the function wizards.

7.1 MegaMillions Numerary

Do you want to calculate lottery numbers? With the first programmable calculators, this was a gimmick, which of course also works in Excel. Well suited to familiarize yourself with the function wizard.

➢ Start a new folder for the following Exercises.

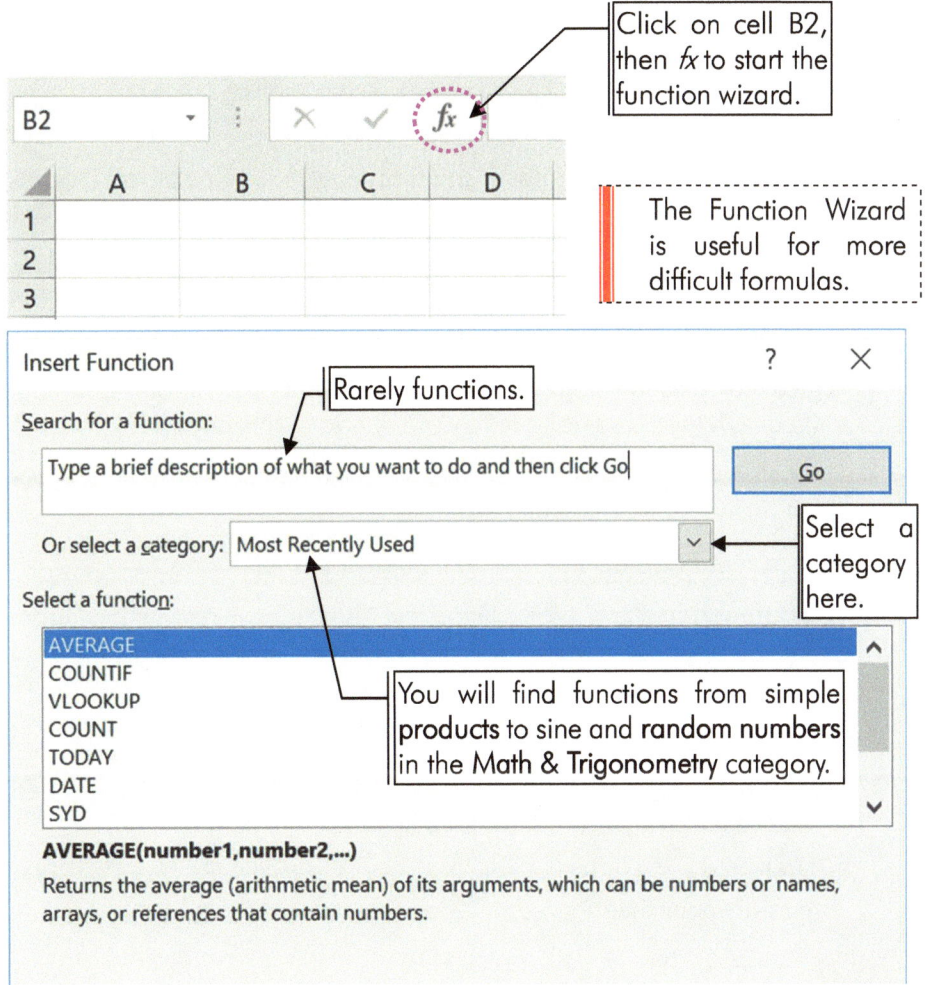

7.1.1 About the Categories

- The most recently used functions are listed under "**Most Recently Used**", initially this is a selection from Excel.
- With "**All**", all available functions are sorted alphabetically.

In addition, all existing formulas are sorted into categories:

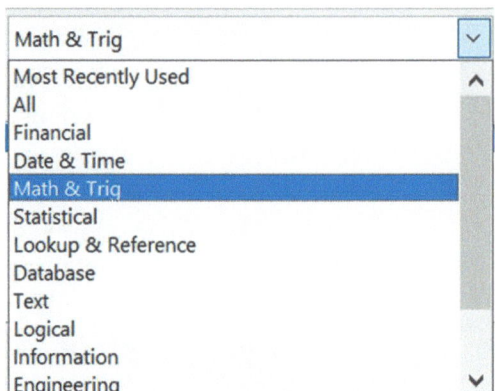

- Formulas for finances such as credit calculation, the yield of a security, depreciation calculations for **Financial**.
- **Date & Time** for time calculations, for example, to calculate the cash discount on a payment date or for shift work plans.
- All sorts of mathematical formulas can be found in **Mathematical & Trigonometric (Math & Trig)**, from sine to rounds, faculty to the root or random number.
- In **Statistical**, you can find statistical formulas such as the frequency of a value, various mean values, the standard deviation, slope, variance or nominal distribution.
- For example, the reference presented at the end of this book can be found in **Lookup & Reference**.
- With **Database**, you can search areas for specific values or total figures in a database.
- For **Text**, you can, for example, convert text to numbers and vice versa or delete spaces in texts or determine identical texts or the number of a character string.
- **Logical** contains functions that lead to an output of TRUE or FALSE, e.g. AND or OR links. Examples follow at the end of this book.
- You can also determine true or false for **Information**, for such as true if a text exists instead of a number.
- Then comes **Engineering**, Cube, Compatibility, and Web.
  - ↳ **Engineering** e.g. for Gaussian functions, conversion from hexadecimal to binary and vice versa, conversion of units of measurement etc.,
  - ↳ **Cube** for Cube Functions,
  - ↳ **Compatibility** is various functions of earlier Excel versions, e.g. Chitest and replaced by ChiQU.test for statistics.
  - ↳ **Web:** Here are three functions, to import specific data from websites into an excel sheet.

7.1.2 The Help

> For Math & Trig., select the function Random Number (Rand).

> At the bottom of the menu you will find a short description and a Hyperlink to more detailed Help for each function:

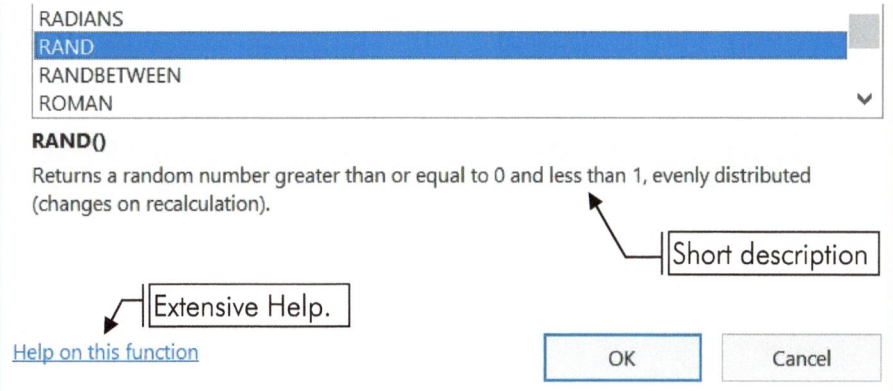

7.1.3 Add Formula

For the lottery numbers, the function alone is not sufficient for the random number, since a number between 0 and 1 is output, but a number between 1 and 49 is required.

> Select "**Rand**" from the category "Math & Trigonometry", then click the Help for this function, follow by OK.

> Insert the **random number** with OK and **add** the formula according to the help text (write manually in the function line as shown):

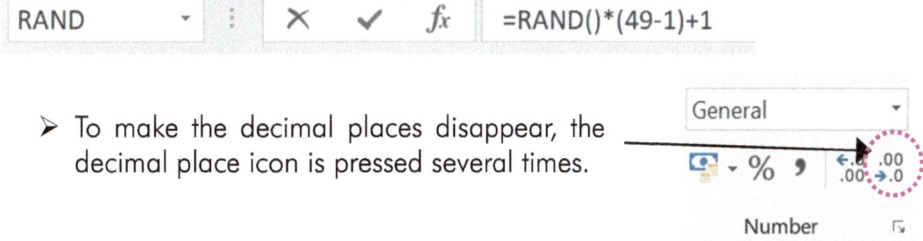

> To make the decimal places disappear, the decimal place icon is pressed several times.

Explanation to the Formula:

♦ the random number between 0 and 1, e.g. 0.34, is multiplied by 49-1, i.e. 48 (we could also insert 48), so that it becomes 0.34*48 = 16.32 +1, by rounding only 16, we have got our first result.

✎ Maximum would be 0.99... times 48 = 47.99... +1 = 49 possibly. Our result is therefore always between 1 and 49.

> Then select the cell, **copy** and paste it into the five following cells so that we get six random numbers at a go.

When inserting a text field, a text was entered and rotated on the rotating arrow. The long text does not disturb the short data values in the cells.

	A	B
1		
2		
3		
4	My MegaMillions Numerary:	28
5		16
6		43
7		31
8		24
9		

New Values:

> ➤ If you want **more Values**, simply select all six cells, copy and paste them into other cells.

> ➤ Or click an empty cell and press the [Del] key, as all values are recalculated each time you delete or insert.

Sorting and conserving Values:

Since new values are calculated for each insert, the numbers cannot simply be copied and pasted.

- ♦ By simply copying and pasting, the formulas would be copied as well, so the values would be changed with each new paste.

- ♦ It would be possible to conserve the numbers by copying them with **Paste content**:

  - ✥ Copy original values, then select another six cells, right-click on them and select **Paste Values** from the drop-down menu, see the figure below.

  - ✥ Then reduce the decimal places.

7.1.4 Fix Results

You can write the date using the conserved values and thus determine the lottery numbers for the following draws, for instance:

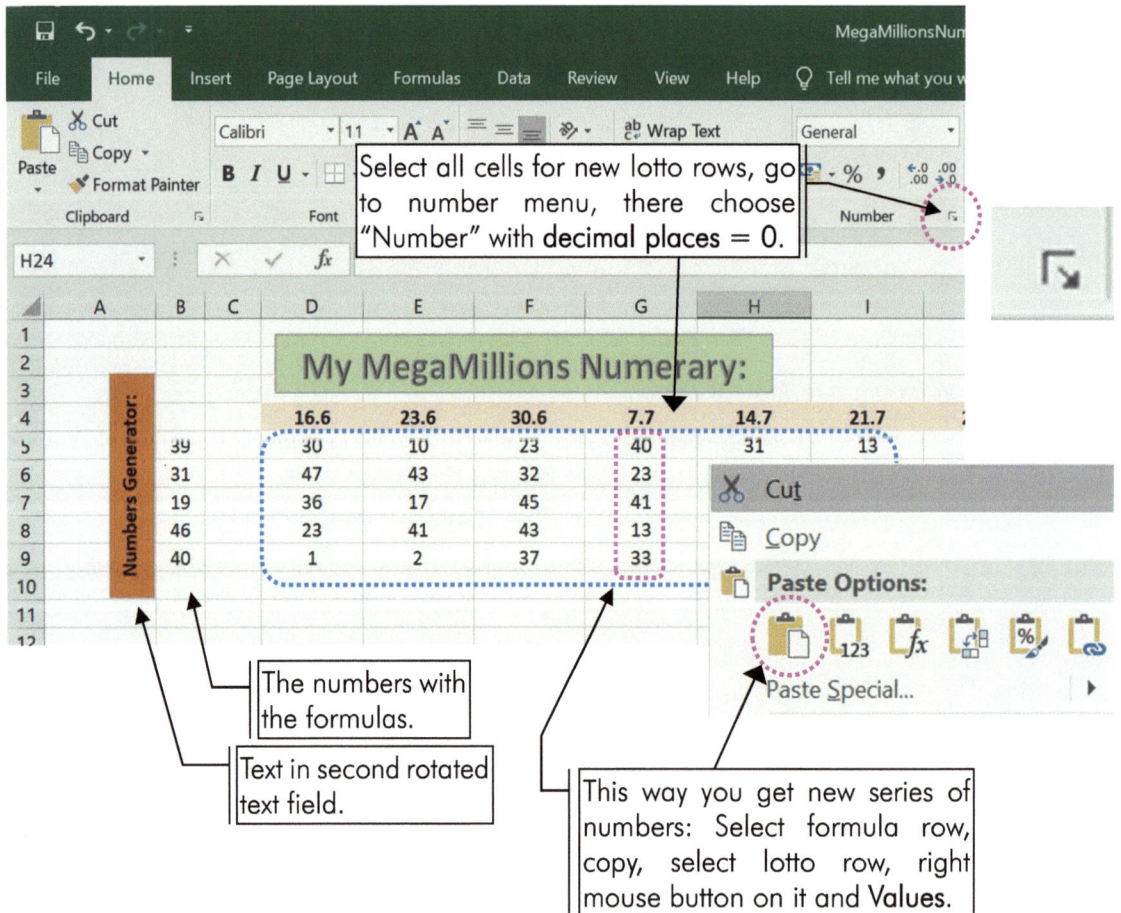

7.1.5 The Smart Tags

For some actions, such as inserting, a small Icon may be displayed. If you click on it, a drop-down list with the most important actions opens, corresponding to the previously selected command.

It is also possible to insert only the values, retain the formatting of the original or adjust it to the target cells.

> ➢ Copy the calculated lotto numbers again, then **paste them normally** in another column:

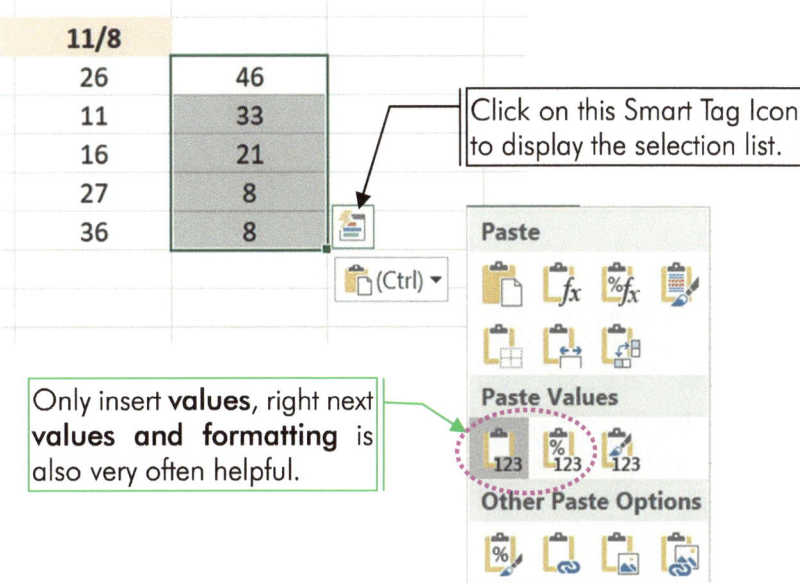

> ➢ You can only insert the values, but you still have the formula numbers in the working memory and could immediately create further new lotto number series.

> ➢ Finally, use **Format Transfer** to import the formatting of the lottery numbers; the reduced decimal places would also be adjusted.

This makes these Smart Tags even more practical.

7.2 Depreciation

You want to calculate the depreciation for accounting purposes or the value loss of an investment? There are Formulas for this too. In this exercise, we want to calculate the loss in value of a motor vehicle.

Let's take the following Sample data:

- ◆ Purchase price $ 35,000,
- ◆ Total useful life of 15 years,
- ◆ a personal useful life of six years with a residual value after these 6 years of approximately $ 9,000.

The real loss in value is particularly high at the beginning and then decreases from year to year.

The SYD function (arithmetical-degressive depreciation) is prepared in Excel for this. You can calculate depreciation at constant rates for accounting purposes using function DDB (declining-balance method of depreciation).

Preparation:

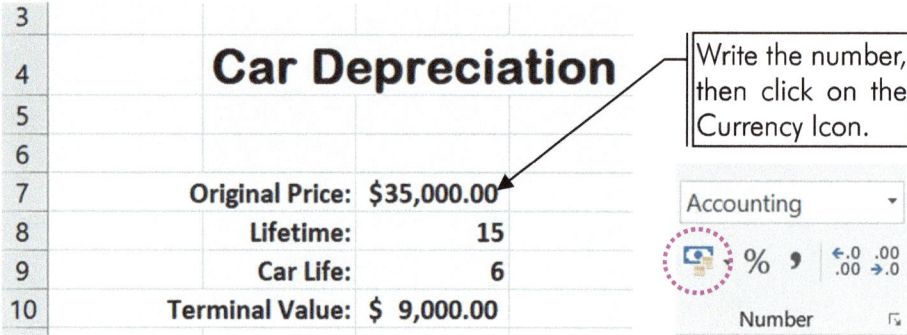

7.2.1 Search Function

We do not want to present you with a few examples in this Training Book, but rather introduce Excel to you in such a way that you can solve your specific tasks with it. As a rule, a suitable function must first be determined.

Supposing you don't know the name of the function. Then you can let Excel **search** for a suitable function.

> Click on an empty cell below the table, then start the **function wizard** and enter "depreciation" at the top of "Search for a function".

> Instructions can be found under "**Financial functions**".

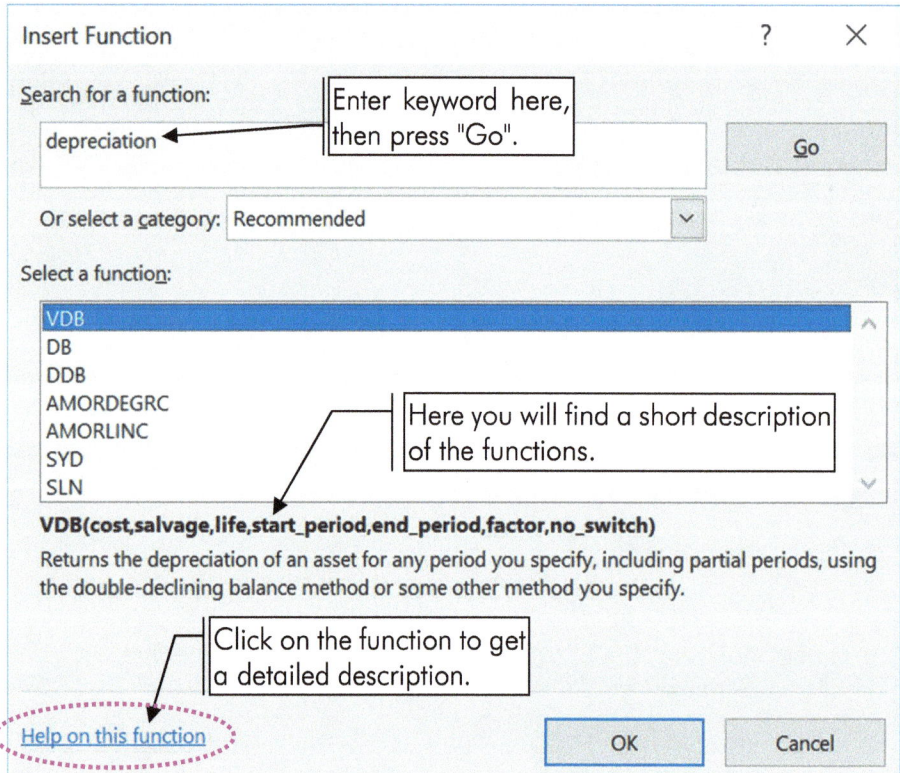

7.2.2 Formula input by Pointing

➢ Click on an empty cell and choose the function SYD (*fx*, either Search or Financial Mathematics and then SYD), then press OK to get to the value Entry as shown.

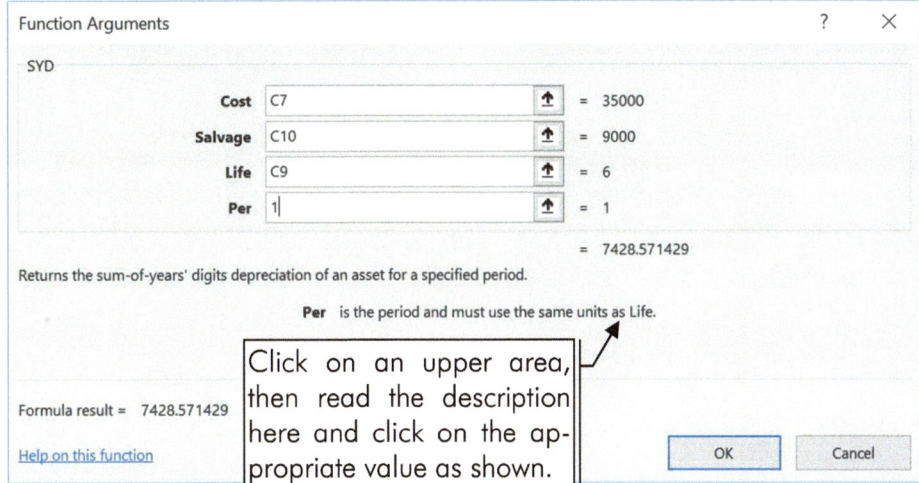

Click on an upper area, then read the description here and click on the appropriate value as shown.

> Excel does not enter the actual value in the function menu but the **Cell**. This has the advantage that you can change the values at any time and the formula result is updated.

7.2.3 Copy Formula

A value for the first year is determined because **Per** = 1 was entered for the first year, the value losses for the following years are still missing.

We copy the formula so that we do not have to set it five times, but the fields are not to be changed so that the same values are always used for the calculation but only the respective year is to be changed.

➢ Therefore, click on the cell with the formula and set the specifications in the function bar to absolute by a preceding $ sign.

=SYD (C$7, C$10, C$9,1)

✎ Since column C always remains the same, it is sufficient this time to set only the **line number** absolutely.

➢ Set "year" in a text field and add the years 1-6 are:

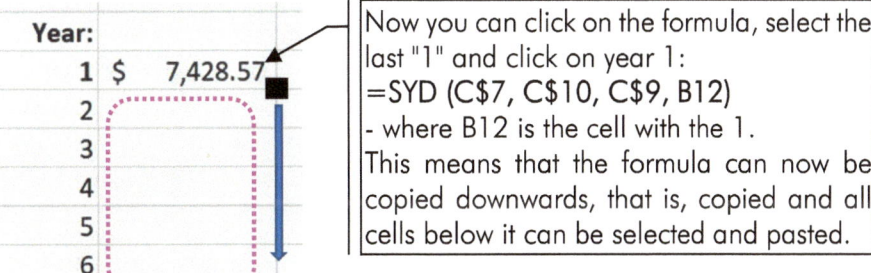

Now you can click on the formula, select the last "1" and click on year 1:
=SYD (C$7, C$10, C$9, B12)
- where B12 is the cell with the 1.
This means that the formula can now be copied downwards, that is, copied and all cells below it can be selected and pasted.

Copy methods: e.g. click the cell with 7,428.57, then [Ctrl]-c for copy, mark the cells below with red line marked and paste with [Ctrl]-v or just pull down on the small box, see above picture.

	A	B	C	D
1				
2				
3				
4		**Car Depreciation**		
5				
6				
7		Original Price:	$ 35,000.00	
8		Lifetime:	15	
9		Car Life:	6	
10		Terminal Value:	$ 9,000.00	
11		Year:	Depreciation:	Terminal Value:
12		1	$ 7,428.57	$27,571.43
13		2	$ 6,190.48	$21,380.95
14		3	$ 4,952.38	$16,428.57
15		4	$ 3,714.29	$12,714.29
16		5	$ 2,476.19	$10,238.10
17		6	$ 1,238.10	$ 9,000.00
18				
19		Control Sum:	$ 26,000.00	

We first calculate the residual value manually by entering the formula by pointing:
=C7-C12
From the next cell D13, we can then copy this formula down to D12-C13.

> Save as "**Car Depreciation**", because we need later again.

The calculated values do not correspond exactly to the actual values because market fluctuations and buyer demand would have to be taken into consideration, for instance, some vehicles with economical engines or certain paints could be demanded higher than other types, or in economically good times 3-year-old used vehicles could be more in demand than 6-year-old ones.

7.2.4 In conclusion

This example shows you the typical steps for creating a calculation with the function wizard:

> Type the known values and search for suitable functions in the Help menu.

> Preparation of the calculation by entering the values,

> Create a formula once with the function wizard and

> If necessary, copy several times, whereby the corresponding values are to be set absolutely.

> Since we can enter +, -, *, / or % using the keyboard, the function wizard only makes sense in practice for difficult formulas. Simple formulas are entered very quickly by pointing.

8. Invoice, Comment, Date

Here are some more practical samples to show the possibilities of the Calculations. First, an Invoice in which the value-added tax is to be displayed.

➢ Start a new **folder** and **save** it as an invoice in our exercise folder right at the beginning.

8.1 The Numerical Formats

➢ Fill in the invoice as follows. Start with an **Invoice** in field **B3**:

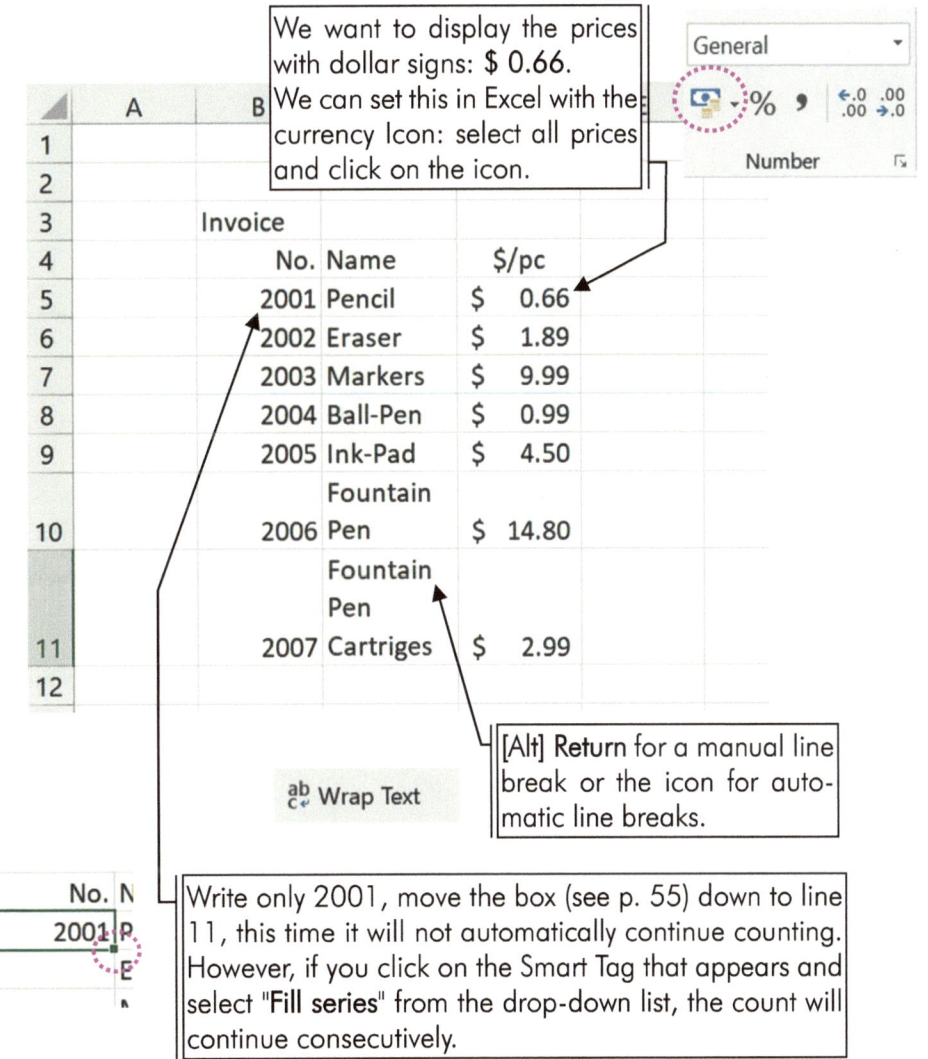

Important number formats are available as Icons:

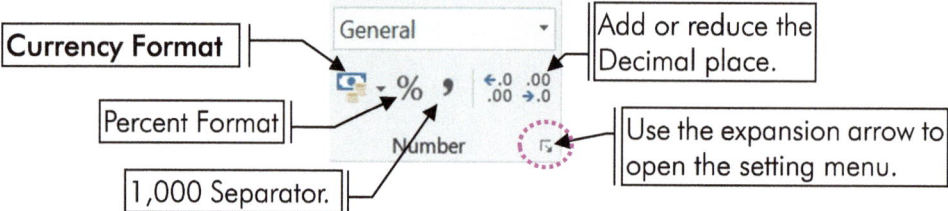

- With the currency format, you can choose from the drop-down list of Pounds, Dollars or Euros, while "More Accounting Formats... " takes you to even more currencies.

  ↳ "**More Number Formats**" opens the same menu as the **expansion arrow**, except that the Accounting Formats for Currencies item is already selected.

Note: only the currency Icon is added here. For information on how to translate between currencies, see page 110.

Other currency Icons or Number Formats can also be formatted using the right **mouse button cells**.

Fill in more, add and format Formulas:

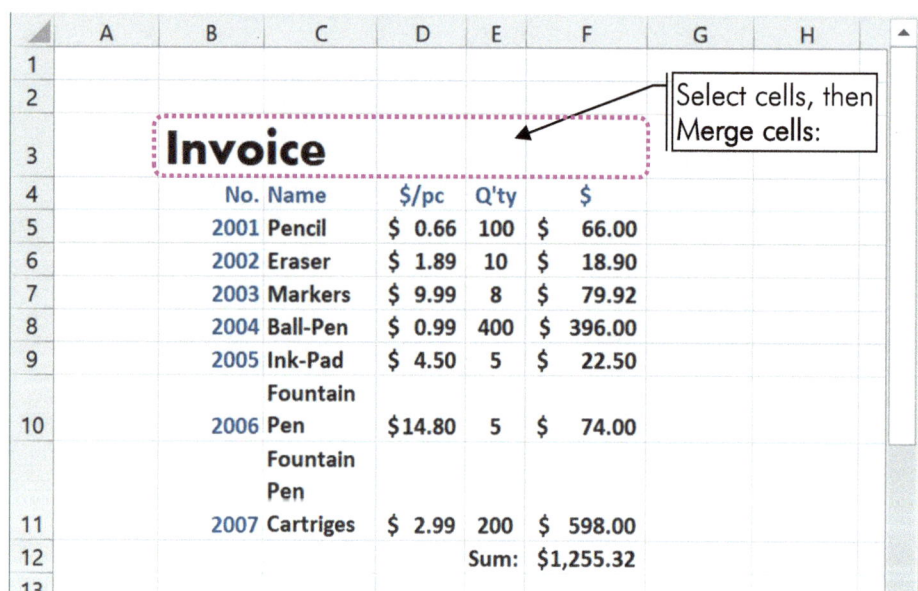

> Add the formula **D5*E5** to **$**,
> then copy or drag the **box down to fill** in the other lines,
> Select the whole column Quantity price and specify **number format $**.

Add Sum:

> Select the cell next to Sum and click the **Sum Icon**.   Σ AutoSum ▾

8.2 The Value Added Tax

We supplement the final block with the Value-Added-Tax and the shipping portion. This is the Sum we just calculated:

	A	B	C	D	E	F
1						
2						
3			Invoice			
4		No.	Name	$/pc	Q'ty	$
5		2001	Pencil	$ 0.66	100	$ 66.00
6		2002	Eraser	$ 1.89	10	$ 18.90
7		2003	Markers	$ 9.99	8	$ 79.92
8		2004	Ball-Pen	$ 0.99	400	$ 396.00
9		2005	Ink-Pad	$ 4.50	5	$ 22.50
10		2006	Fountain Pen	$14.80	5	$ 74.00
11		2007	Fountain Pen Cartriges	$ 2.99	200	$ 598.00
12					Sum:	$ 1,255.32
13					Value-Added Tax:	$ 238.51
					Shipping:	$ 10.00
					Total:	$1,503.83

Either with the "Point": = type, then click on the sum, VAT and shipping part, press + in between or the Sum Icon, then specify the required area.

- We can calculate **percentages** in these two ways:
  - Either with the % sign. Then enter this: = F12*19%
  - or the complete calculation: = F12/100*19.

> Note that we place an equal sign at the beginning so that Excel recognizes the numbers as a Formula. Without "=", Excel displays the formula but does not calculate.

➢ Enter one of the two formulas for VAT.

➢ Enter the **shipping share**, then have the final amount calculated as a Sum:
  - Select the cells from the sum to the final amount and press the sum symbol or
  - double click on the cell next to the final amount, then = type, click on the sum + type VAT + type and click on dispatch and finish with Return.

➢ **Format** the lines as shown.

Add Frame lines, in addition to Fill and Text Color.

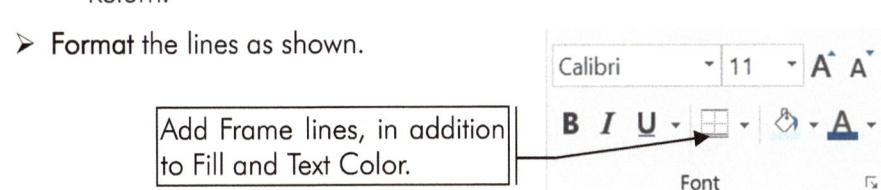

8.3 A Comment

Comments can be added to calculations. This can help you to understand the formulas at a later point in time, or help others to familiarize themselves more quickly with the calculation.

It also allows you to record additional **information**, such as the amount of shipping.

> ➤ Click on the field with $ 10.00 postage and select **Check/New Comment**.

> ↳ This function can also be started with the **right mouse button/insert comment**.

Insert Comment:

- ♦ Enter the above text in the **text window** that appears.
    - ↳ The border at the **drag point** can be increased or decreased by holding down the mouse button.
- ➤ Finally, **click another cell**. The comment is saved with the Excel table.

Comments are indicated by small triangles:

- ♦ If you now move the mouse slowly over the field with the comment, the **comment will be displayed**.

You can also insert texts from other programs into an Excel comment field. Simply select the text, copy, switch to Excel and place the cursor in the comment, then choose Paste.

8.3.1 Change Comments

- ♦ You can change comments in this way:
    - ↳ **right mouse** button anywhere above the cell with the comment, then **Edit the comment**:
    - ↳ In this drop-down menu, you can also **delete** a comment.

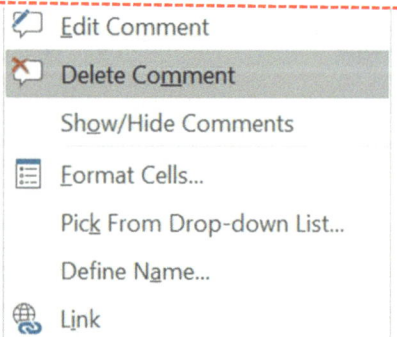

The comment opens again in;

- to **correct** the text or with the
- **[Delete] key** to **delete** the comment completely if the comment frame is selected or
- to **select** the whole **text**, cut ([Ctrl]-X) and paste it into another cell with **Paste Comment** and [Ctrl]-V.

The latter allows you to **move** a comment to another location.

- The "**Show All Comments**" button under Review always displays comments, regardless of whether they are selected.

8.4 Insert the current Date

Let us add the invoice date. This is possible in several ways.

Insert unchangeable Date:

[Ctrl]-[Shift]-[;]

- **jot down** the date: e.g. 29/08/2018. Advantage: this value remains unchanged.
  - This can be done faster with the keyboard shortcut **[Ctrl]-[Shift]-[;]**.
  - With **[Ctrl]-[Shift]-[:]** the **current time** is inserted.

Insert the date that is automatically updated:

- Open formula editor (fx Icon)/category Date & Time, insert **NOW**.

- Add to the amount below:

> If you use the "**Now**" function, the date is updated automatically. For invoices, store a print-out to retain the invoice date, or better still use [Ctrl]-[Shift]-[;].

8.4.1 Calculations with Date

We give the customer a **2% discount** if payment is made within 14 days. And so that the customer does not have to calculate the last payment date, this will be done in Excel.

There are numerous formulas for the Date and Time. The simplest method is as follows:

Enter the formulas as shown.

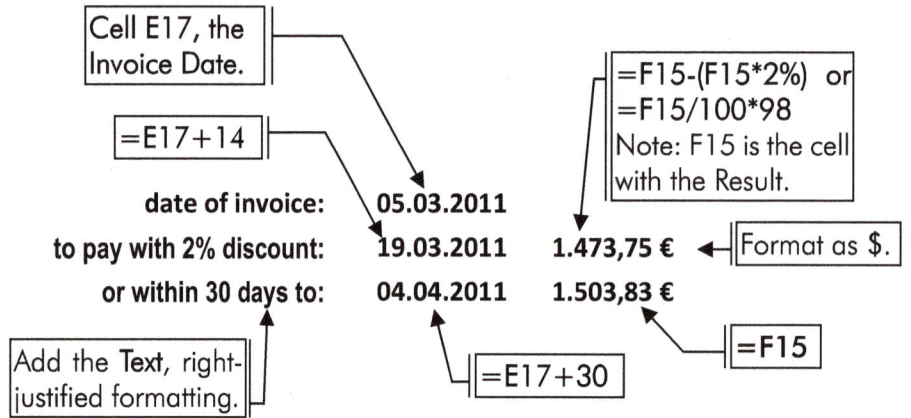

We refer to the **date cell E17** instead of using a function like "Today" so that the date would not be updated and thus changed later. With "Today", the formula ="Today "+14.

- Calculations with **Date** are generally only possible if
  - Date values are enclosed in **quotation marks** and if the
  - Cells are set to a **Date format**:
  - right mouse button over the Cell, then **Format cells** and select a **Date format** on the Number index card.

The invoice completed so far:

	A	B	C	D	E	F	G
1							
2							
3			**Invoice**				
4		No.	Name	$/pc	Q'ty	$	
5		2001	Pencil	$ 0.66	100	$ 66.00	
6		2002	Eraser	$ 1.89	10	$ 18.90	
7		2003	Markers	$ 9.99	8	$ 79.92	
8		2004	Ball-Pen	$ 0.99	400	$ 396.00	
9		2005	Ink-Pad	$ 4.50	5	$ 22.50	
10		2006	Fountain Pen	$14.80	5	$ 74.00	
11		2007	Fountain Pen Cartriges	$ 2.99	200	$ 598.00	
12					Sum:	$ 1,255.32	
13					Value-Added Tax:	$ 238.51	
14					Shipping:	$ 10.00	
15					Total:	$1,503.83	
16							
17							
18					date of invoice:	29/06/2018	
19					to pay with 2% discount:	13/07/2018	$1,473.75
20					or within 30 days to:	29/07/2018	$1,503.83
21							

8.5 Rationalize Invoice

Of course, you have to write such invoices more often and do not want to enter the designations, article numbers and prices every time. This would be a use case for **MS Access** or another database or accounting program. With a simple makeshift for Excel:

- Add some blank lines above, then use **Insert Forms** to set a **rectangle** for the address above.
- Right mouse button on this rectangle and **edit text**, then enter a customer address.
- You could also add a Letterhead at the top with such a frame.
- Switch off the panel for the frame and also set the line or an inconspicuous line, e.g. a *dotted line*.
- **Copy** the invoice including all articles with numbers, prices and formulas (i.e. the whole line) to a new spreadsheet.
- If an article is added later, copy it to this spreadsheet as well.
- Rename this sheet to **Article**.

This Sheet is our data collection. Therefore, proceed as follows for a new Invoice:

- Copy this **complete invoice** to another sheet so that all formatted texts are transferred.
- Delete **Items** not ordered and update Date.
  - If the whole line is selected in this way, the following lines will be moved in, therefore, this will disallow any gap.
- **Ad**just **quantities**, and the new invoice is ready.

You are welcome to try this out as described as an Exercise:

- As described, copy all articles to a new sheet, add a new article to **break bread** there, rename the sheet to the article.
- Then copy all articles on a new **sheet**, delete not needed, adjust quantities in order to change both the address and date.
  - A new sheet can be used for each new invoice so that the old invoices are retained.
  - As soon as there are too many invoices, such as after one month, then save the folder as Invoice-Year-Month and start a new folder.

Of course, it is also possible to copy and paste the calculation into a Word template for your invoices.

9. A Budgetary Planning

Do you want to keep a clear overview of your Income and Expenses? Let's try this with Excel. *This calculation is only exemplary*. To make this a concrete application, you would have to enter your tax rate and possible tax allowances and other deductions.

> Create a New folder and save as **Budget Planning**.

> Let's start with your **Income**, that is, your Salary, from which of course some deductions have to be calculated:

	Salary Calculation				Formulas:
Row:				Januar	
3	Gross	Gross income		3.000,00	= Cell D3
4					
5	Tax	Income tax	22%	660,00	=D3*C5 (=Zelle D5)
6		Additional tax % from income tax	7,5%	49,50	=D5*C6
7		Church tax % from income tax	8%	52,80	=D5*C7
8		Sum Tax:		762,30	=D5+D6+D7
9					
10	Insurances	Health Insurance	14,9%	447,00	=$D$3*C10
11		Pension Insurance	19,5%	585,00	=$D$3*C11
12		Care Insurance	1,7%	51,00	=$D$3*C12
13		unemployment insurance	6,5%	195,00	=$D$3*C13
14		Sum Insurances:		1.278,00	=D10+D11+D12+D13
15					
16	Others	Other Income			
17					
18					
19	Net	Sum:		1.598,70	=D3-D8-D14 +D16
20					

> Since the tax rates are constantly changing, we enter their values with the % sign in a separate column. This means that the records can be changed at any time without having to change the formulas.

✎ The reference to the cell is sufficient if you type % to the value.

9.1 Automatically Fill in with Row

We do not need to enter the **Months** ahead separately in the following columns. Excel does this for us using the Fill function.

Row with the Mouse:

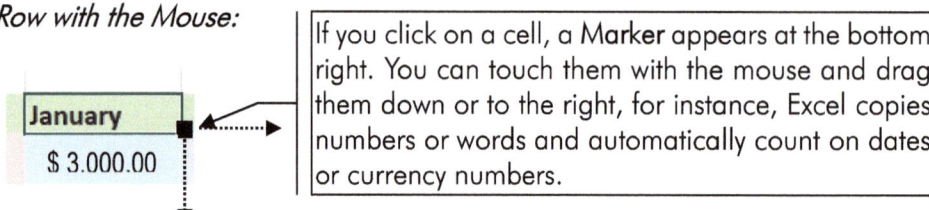

If you click on a cell, a **Marker** appears at the bottom right. You can touch them with the mouse and drag them down or to the right, for instance, Excel copies numbers or words and automatically count on dates or currency numbers.

➢ **Click** on the January Cell and drag the box to the right to "December".

The Row Dialog Box:

This function with the Mouse works for standard cases such as the date or a consecutive line number. This can be set specifically in the dialog box, which we have already examined.

When using the menu, first **select** the cells to be filled, including the cell with the first value:

➢ Press Undo, then select approximately the same number of cells from January on to the right.

➢ Then select **Fill/Series** on the far right at Start.

↳ Down, right, etc. would repeat the same value as with type Linear in the following menu.

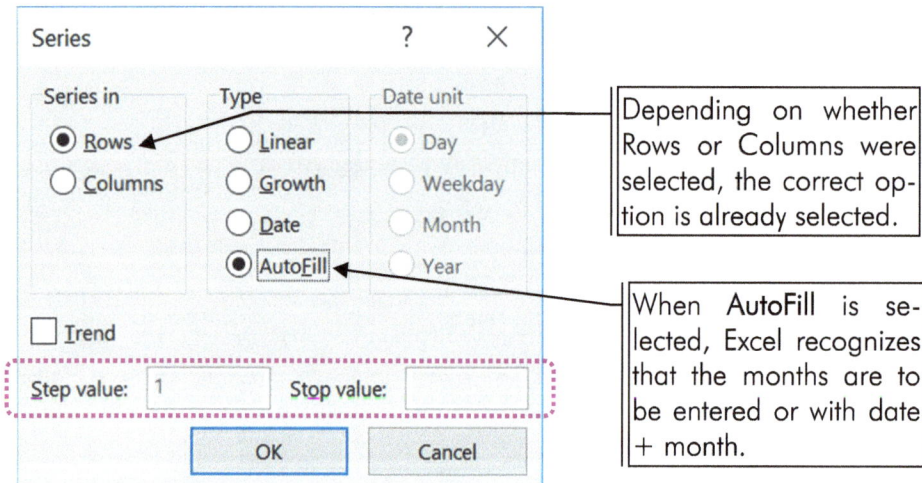

Depending on whether Rows or Columns were selected, the correct option is already selected.

When **AutoFill** is selected, Excel recognizes that the months are to be entered or with date + month.

About the "Step value":

- ♦ **1** (more precisely +1) means: continue counting: January, February ... or 1996, 1997.... or €22, €23 ...
- ♦ **0** would fill with the unchanged initial value,
- ♦ **-1** counts in the different direction: January, December, November... or 1996, 1995, 1994...
- ♦ **2** counts in steps of 2: January, March, May ... or 1996, 1998...; accordingly you can continue counting with 10 in intervals of ten or enter any other values, e.g. 0.1.

9.2 Fill in automatically to the right

We're moving on. The salary is the same for each month, and the formulas should also be copied to all other monthly columns.

Here, too, we let the Fill function do the work for us.

> Since you want the percentages in **column C** to remain the same when you fill in the form, place a **$ sign** before C, for example, =D3*$C5. Therefore, the Sums can remain unchanged.

> Now **select** all cells except the month in the January-column.

> Since the same values are to be used in this case, it is necessary to drag to the right from the box.

January
3000

> ✋ Oops - but not? Excel had continued to count the gross salary. Simply pull it separately to the right again.

> Finally, the salary values sometimes change somewhat, that is, due to more being earned through overtime in a few months or a Christmas bonus being added:

	A	B	C	D	E	F
1	**Salary Calculation**					
2			Value	January	February	March
3	**Gross**	Gross income		$ 3,000.00	$ 3,100.00	$ 3,150.00
4						
5	**Tax**	Income tax	22%	$ 660.00	$ 682.00	$ 693.00
6		Additional tax % from income tax	7.50%	$ 49.50	$ 51.15	$ 51.98
7		Church tax % from income tax	8%	$ 52.80	$ 54.56	$ 55.44
8		Sum Tax:		$ 762.30	$ 787.71	$ 800.42
9						
10	**Insurances**	Health Insurance	14.90%	$ 447.00	$ 447.00	$ 447.00
11		Pension Insurance	19.50%	$ 585.00	$ 585.00	$ 585.00
12		Care Insurance	1.70%	$ 51.00	$ 51.00	$ 51.00
13		unemployment insurance	6.50%	$ 195.00	$ 195.00	$ 195.00
14		Sum Insurances:		$ 1,278.00	$ 1,278.00	$ 1,278.00
15						
16	**Others**	Other Income			$ 90.00	$ 100.00
17						
18						
19	**Net**			$ 959.70	$ 1,124.29	$ 1,171.59
20						
21						

9.3 Document with Comments

We augment some of the other Income for all unscheduled financial transactions:

> For **additional Revenues**, enter $90 in February and $100 in March, then format $ as currency.

Others	Other Income		$ 90.00	$ 100.00
Net	Sum:	$ 959.70	$ 1,124.29	$ 1,171.59

> Register how the calculated revenues **change** automatically.

It is impossible to always insert a new line for such rare events. However, we document this with a **commentary** so that we can still recognize what it is all about:

> Click on cell $90,00, then add the following text with the **right mouse button comment** (chapter 8.3): "Flea market on February 14, 18".

> At $100.00 add the following comment: "from Grandma on her Birthday".

Please note:

- if a commentary exists is indicated by a small ⌐ one in the upper right cell.
- The comment itself is displayed as soon as you move the mouse over this cell.
- Right mouse button over the cell with the comment and you can edit existing comments. The size of the comment window can also be adjusted with the mouse at the Handle points.

This could be the concept:

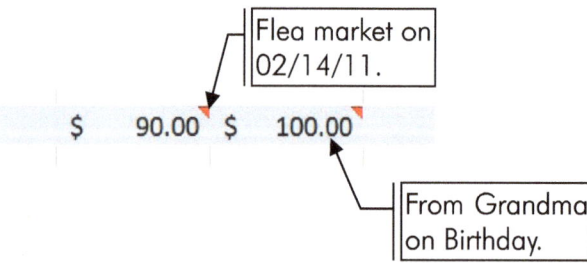

- With **comments**, you can immediately recognize what it is about.
- For more frequent items, you can add **new Lines** or calculate them on separate sheets.

9.4 Add Overview

Add an Overview for the whole year to the far right:

	K	L	M	N	O	P	Q
1							
2	August	September	October	November	December	Sum:	Overview:
3	$ 3,000.00	$ 3,000.00	$ 3,000.00	$ 3,000.00	$ 3,800.00	37,050.00 €	Sum Income
4							
5	$ 660.00	$ 660.00	$ 660.00	$ 660.00	$ 836.00	$ 8,151.00	
6	$ 49.50	$ 49.50	$ 49.50	$ 49.50	$ 62.70	$ 611.33	
7	$ 52.80	$ 52.80	$ 52.80	$ 52.80	$ 66.88	$ 652.08	
8	$ 762.30	$ 762.30	$ 762.30	$ 762.30	$ 965.58	$ 9,414.41	Sum Tax
9							
10	$ 447.00	$ 447.00	$ 447.00	$ 447.00	$ 447.00	$ 5,364.00	
11	$ 585.00	$ 585.00	$ 585.00	$ 585.00	$ 585.00	$ 7,020.00	
12	$ 51.00	$ 51.00	$ 51.00	$ 51.00	$ 51.00	$ 612.00	
13	$ 195.00	$ 195.00	$ 195.00	$ 195.00	$ 195.00	$ 2,340.00	
14	$ 1,278.00	$ 1,278.00	$ 1,278.00	$ 1,278.00	$ 1,278.00	$ 15,336.00	Sum Insurances
15							
16						190.00 €	Sum Others
17							
18							
19	$ 959.70	$ 959.70	$ 959.70	$ 959.70	$ 1,556.42	$ 12,489.60	Sum Net
20							

The Formulas are very simple:

- In P3, simply press the Sum Icon. Copy this Sum to the following cells, making sure that the column with the percentages is not counted, that is, columns D to O only.
- In the Overview, only add the appropriate text entry for the respective Sums.

If you run this evaluation over several years, you could copy the annual overviews to a separate spreadsheet. Before copying, of course, the year numbers should be added to the Headings.

- Create an **Annual Overview**. Insert a new spreadsheet, first copy the Overview column as the first column, add the year number in the Sum column and then copy it next to it.
- The calculated values are not copied, they have been deleted again and indicated by pointing: click on the new sheet e.g. salary cell, = type, then click on the value with the mouse on the Revenue sheet and confirm with Return.

Later, these values could be used to display and evaluate the salary and tax development, e.g. as a diagram. Of course, expenditure should not be missing either.

	Overview: Sum 2018:
Sum Income:	37,050.00 €
Sum Tax:	9,414.41 €
Sum Insurances:	2,340.00 €
Sum Others:	190.00 €
Net Sum:	12,489.60 €

9.5 The Expenditures

In the case of Expenditure, it is advisable to set up several **smaller and manageable areas**, e.g. for housing finance or for regular subsistence expenses which are negotiated by means of Subtotals. This makes it easier to detect errors.

➤ Create and Format the following Table:

Expenses 2018			January	February
	Living	Hire Carges:		
		Additional Carges:		
		Power Costs:		
		Sum Living:		
	Household	Eating:		
		Drinking:		
		Clothes:		
		Cleaning Agents:		
		Household Aids:		
		Sum Household:		
	Insurances	Private Liability:		
		Live Assurance:		
		Household Insurance:		
		Sum Insurances:		
	Car	Insurance:		
		Car Tax:		
		Service Costs:		
		Fuel Costs:		
		Sum Car:		
	Aquirements	Music Equipment:	1,299.00 €	
		TV:		
		Furniture:		
		Others:		
		Sum Aquirements:		
		TOTAL:		

Subtotals help to avoid over-long formulas and provide over-viewable for easily controllable intermediate results.

Comment: Hi-Fi mini system, bought at Hi-Fi-Market.

➤ Enter **values** and the appropriate formulas for the **subtotals**, so that only the subtotals have to be added for the **final amount** (specify by pointing).

➤ **Name** the sheets to match your **Income** and **Expenses**.

➤ Add the total to the **annual overview**, then calculate the income minus the total expenditure.

Part 3

CALCULATE INTEREST RATE

Financial calculations manually and with the formulas

10. Credit Calculation

First, we will calculate the repayment for the Loan itself to illustrate the principle of the Invoice. In the end, we will use the **PMT** function that Excel provides for regular payments.

> Start a **new Folder** and
> enter the following **Values**:

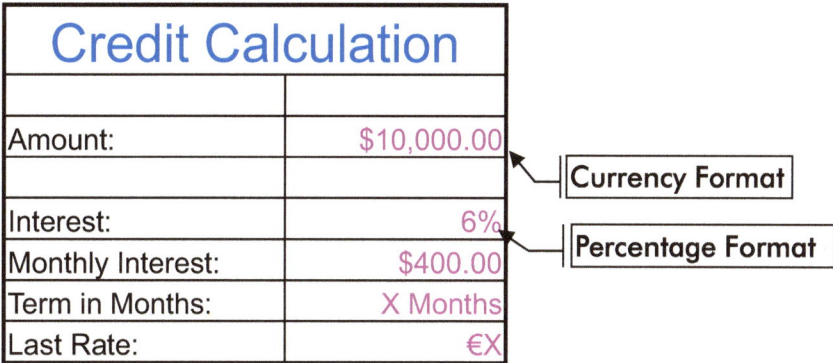

10.1 The Principle of the Calculation

We will first calculate a good exercise for the automatic completion of the installments to be paid.

- It's definite:
  - the desired credit amount of -$ 10,000.00
  - the interest rate of 6% and
  - the desired repayment rate of -$ 400, per month.
- The **Runtime** is to be determined from these values,
  - with a little less debt every month,
  - the Interest to be paid,
  - so that the repayment share is constantly increasing.

10.2 The Calculation

Add on a **second Sheet**:

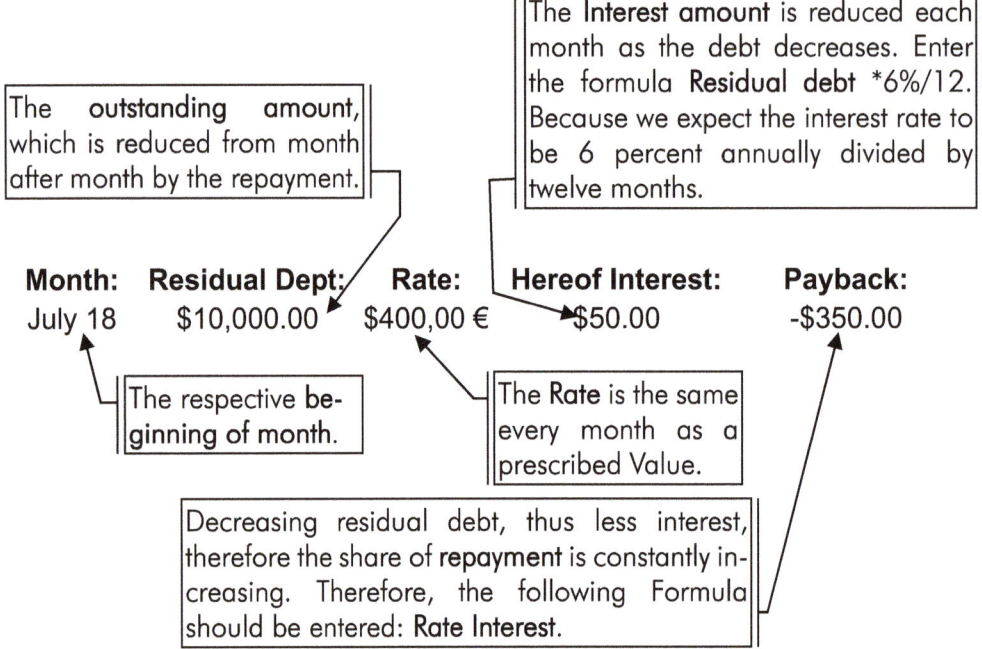

The easiest way to specify all formulas is to point to "=".

10.3 The second Line

It's extremely important:

Also, here the Input by pointing proves itself:

- Open the cell for the new residual debt (9,650) by double-clicking, = type, then click on the residual debt €10,000, type minus and click on the repayment.
  - ✎ If you use negative payback ($-350) use the formula with plus.
  - ✎ This causes the coordinates to be inserted instead of the values so that the formulas can be copied relatively.

> During copying, the month is to continue counting, but the rate remains the same each month and the residual debt is to be calculated relatively according to the formula. Therefore, we will expand the cells separately downwards so that the appropriate option can be selected.

10.4 Completion

We want to add the remaining lines as automatically as possible. Now you have to consider that all columns should be continued relatively, therefore, only the value at **Rate** remains unchanged.

> Click on the **Rate** and drag it down with the mouse. If only the Rate down the column is extended, the value remains unchanged.

The remaining Columns:

In the case of **Residual debt**, we are one line lower due to the Formula.

> Subtract **Month** and **Residual Debt** separately, then add **Interest** and **Repayment** together.

Now the lines are filled out as desired:

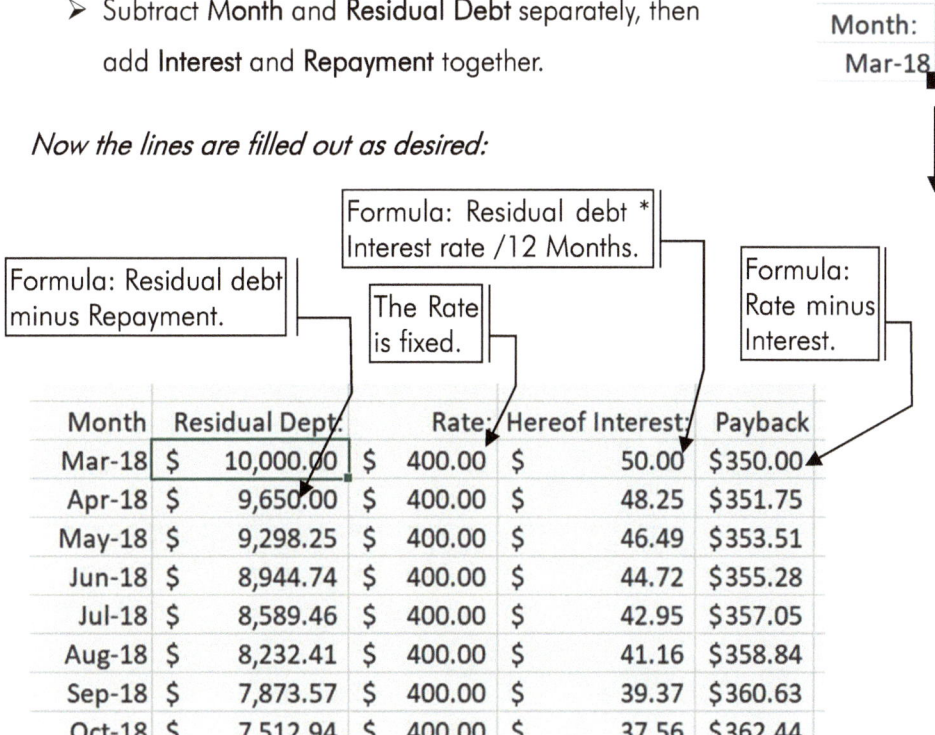

Add more lines until a negative residual debt amount appears:

> Now we can expand **all columns down at once**.
>> Excel would only continue to pay at the **Rate**, therefore, simply expand it separately with the mouse downwards.

As the outstanding debt decreases, the proportion of the repayment, therefore, increases monthly and the expiration is reached on a reversal of negative debt values. The full installment is no longer payable in the previous month.

Month	Residual Dept		Rate		Hereof Interest	Payback
Mar-20	$	1,098.82	$ 400.00	$	5.49	$394.51
Apr-20	$	704.31	$ 400.00	$	3.52	$396.48
May-20	$	307.83	$ 400.00	$	1.54	$398.46
Jun-20	$	-90.63	$ 401.00	$	-0.45	$401.45

This month, the debt is converted into a credit balance, so the **last Rate** in June 2020 is a manual invoice: €307.83 (Residual debt) + €1.54 (interest) = €309.37. The entire loan including the Interest would then be repaid. *Correct the last payoff to this value (enter formula)!*

10.5 Count Rows

Final question: how **many months** have been repaid?

> ➢ First, **delete** the months with negative repayment.

In this simple case, you could click on the last line, read the **line number** on the left and subtract the title lines from it, resulting in 27 lines, i.e. 27 months of repayment. Or **mark the months** and read their number in the status bar at the bottom.

Of course, there is a formula for this, which is sometimes quite practical:

> ➢ Click the next line after May-20 and click the *fx* icon.
>> ✵ Select the formula **Count**. You may find these under "last used", otherwise under **All** or in the **Statistics** group.
>
> ➢ After OK, hold down the mouse button and **select** all cells that are to be counted as soon as you reach the following Window.

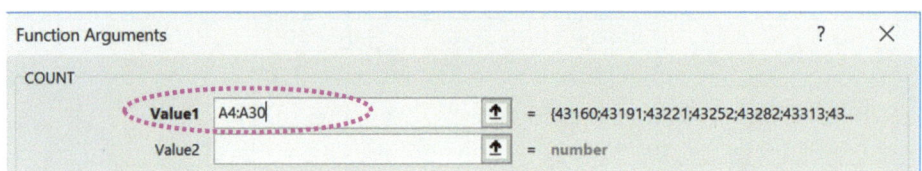

> ➢ Finally, change the **number format** for the result from date to a normal number until 27 is displayed.
>
> ➢ Extend further down and add the text "Number of Months", set the calculated value 27 absolute: =COUNT ($A$4: $A$30), then cut and paste next to it.

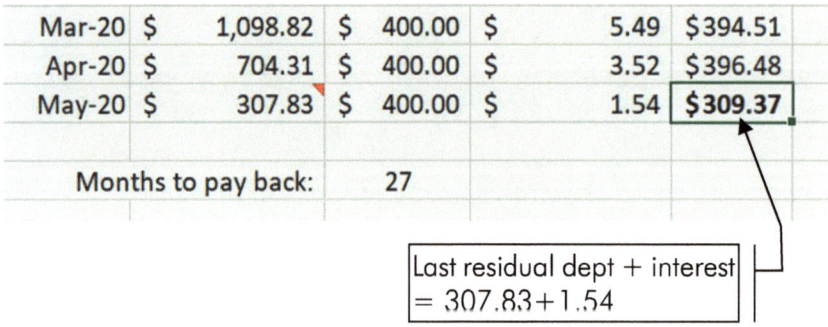

10.6 Values Vary

On the second calculation page, you could extend the table down, then enter different loan amounts and installments at the top and view the repayment period based on the conversion to negative numbers.

> Unfortunately, the manual calculation per table cannot automatically extend or shorten the number of months.

To get a really flexible calculation, a suitable formula from Excel is needed.

11. The Financial Formula PMT

This manual calculation is a bit time-consuming, especially if you want to change the duration or amounts. Good to practice and to understand the principle. Let's try the same with the Excel function **PMT** for regular payment.

You can use the **PMT** function to calculate the monthly payment for both credit and savings. The difference lies only in the <u>Sign</u>. Interest and repayment or savings are taken into consideration.

> We use a **third spreadsheet** to keep the exercise in a workbook.

> **Copy** the overview from sheet 1 to sheet 3 so that we don't have to rewrite everything.

> **Rename** the sheets appropriately, for example, to Result Credit, Calculation Credit, and PMT Credit.

This is what Table 3 should look like for the time being:

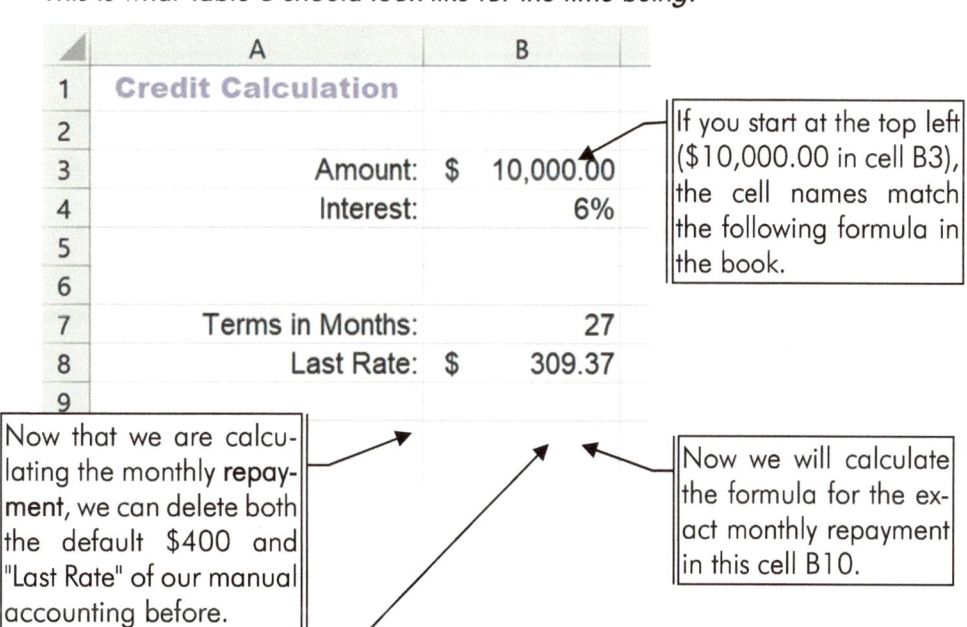

> Click on the cell, press the **formula icon** fx and select
> Select the formula **PMT** in the categories "All" or "**Financial**".

11.1 The Entry Menu

After OK, you can enter the values for the formula:

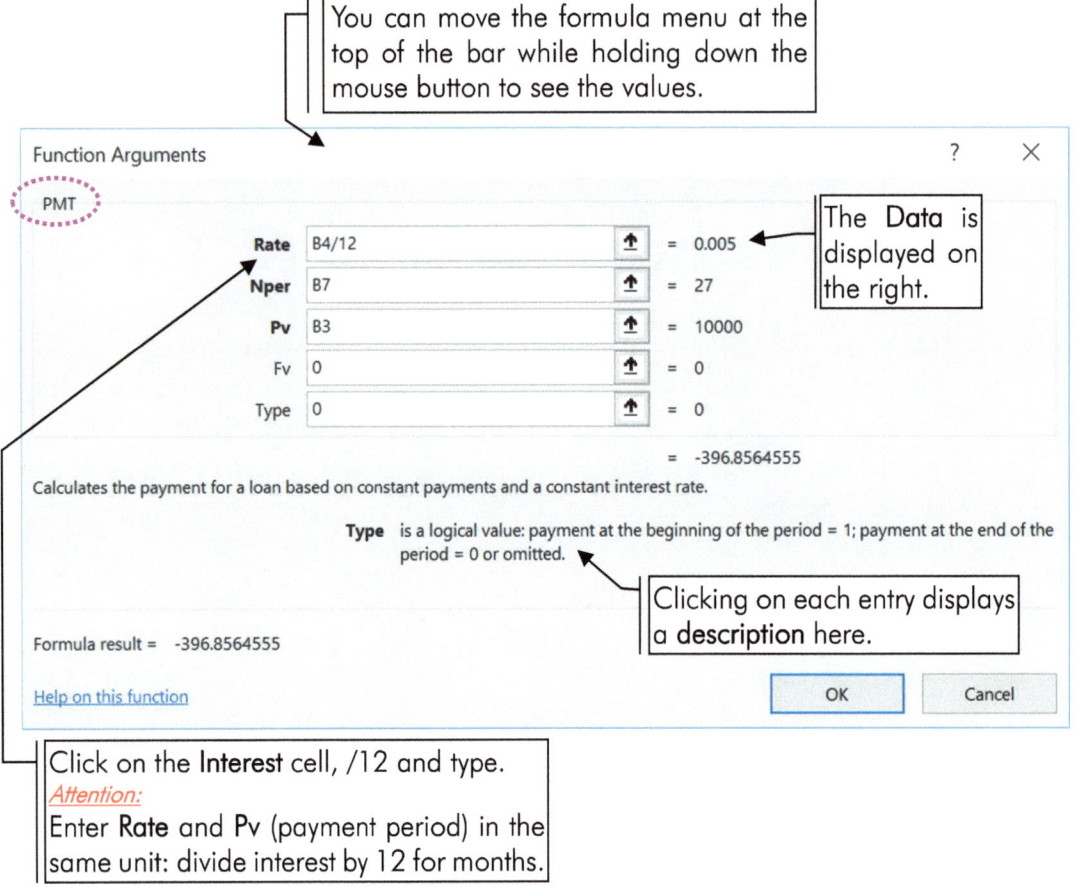

Click on the **Interest** cell, /12 and type.
Attention:
Enter **Rate** and **Pv** (payment period) in the same unit: divide interest by 12 for months.

➢ **Move** the menu and enter the values by **pointing** with the mouse.

11.2 Explanations

- **Rate** is the interest rate, please divide by 12, because we need the interest per month, since usually the

- Payment period **Nper** in months has to be entered.

> Of course, you can also enter the interest per year and the term in years as well, but be careful: this is a frequent **source of errors** if the information does not match!

- The credit amount is entered for **Pv** (for cash value):
  - For a loan, the loan amount and Fv = 0
  - Note that when saving, Pv is zero and Fv is the desired final amount.

- **Fv** (future value) is the target final value,
  - for a loan usually 0,
  - and the desired savings sum for a savings scheme.
  - If no Fv is entered, it is considered 0.

- **Type** is the due date, see the following table.
    - If you specify the payment period and the interest in another unit, for example, in **Years**, the due date F automatically applies to these periods, for example, with 0 at the end of the year.

Type	Payment Due:
0	At month end (no entry = 0)
1	At the beginning of the month

11.3 The Function

If you confirm with OK, the following function is inserted:

= PMT (B4/12; B7; B3;0;0)

The installment amount of $ -396.86 is calculated.

- A slight difference to our result, which results from the fact that
    - Excel does not insert the last equalization month,
    - but a constant value from the first to the last month.

If you want to change the function directly:

PMT(Rate; Nper; Pv; Fv; Type) is called:
Interest; Payment period; Present value; Future value; Maturity.

> Also, note that you should use the **same time units** for installment and Nper, that is, usually divide the interest for months by twelve.

Hint:

- **PMT** provides the monthly amount to be paid.
- **Terms in Months** (the term in months) indicates how often you have to pay or save the desired amount.
    - Multiply both values in another cell and you get the **total amount** you have to pay.

Complete the Credit Calculation with the formula PMT:

	A	B
1	**Credit Calculation**	
2		
3	Amount:	$ 10,000.00
4	Interest:	6%
5		
6		
7	Terms in Months:	27
8	Last Rate:	$ 309.37
9		
10	Monthly Rate:	$ -396.86
11		
12	Sum of Payments:	$ -10,715.12
13		

Now you can insert any values desired:

> Determine the values for loan sums of $20,000 and $300,000 and for an interest rate of only 4 percent or twice as long maturity.

With PMT you can therefore not only calculate the monthly amount to pay off a loan but also simulate various scenarios.

11.4 Excel Credit Template

You can also find Excel templates with **File/New**, credit calculation templates with the formula PMT and many other extras, two examples:

- **Balloon Payment Loan**:
    - If the "loan amount" is changed, the monthly amount, not the period is adjusted.

- **Mortgage Payment Calculator**:
    - Note the repayment table. You can change this value on the overview page. The Purchase price field is not linked to this value and must also be adjusted manually.
    - If the loan amount changes, the monthly amount rather than the period is adjusted in the repayment table.

- If a template is protected against changes, you can unprotect it directly under Start in the **Format** drop-down menu: **Cancel Sheet Protection** (unless this is blocked by a password).

12. A Savings Bond

With PMT, we are now also going the other way round. *We don't pay off debts, we save.*

Note, however, only the desired final amount can be specified with PMT and the monthly contribution to be paid can be determined.

It is not possible with PMT to determine what final amount you would receive with a certain monthly savings amount over a certain period of time. For this purpose, there is the formula FV, which is introduced afterward.

12.1 Saved Amount

> Use a new sheet for this exercise. Calculate what monthly savings would have to be paid at the selected interest rate in three years to save the final amount:

Saving with PMT	
Pre Payment:	
Saving Amount:	
Interest:	5 %
Term in Months:	3
Last Amount:	$10.000

Calculate the required saved amount.

> Try to use **PMT** to get the monthly rate.

Notes:

- Excel also outputs a negative value in this respect.

> Whenever you pay amounts they are always negative.

- Payment should be made at the **beginning of the month** to earn interest on the money.

To Entry:

- **Rate**: divide the interest rate in percentage by 12 months.
- **Nper**: click on the cell with the payment period and take 12 months, because the period is given in years and we want to calculate the monthly amount to be paid.
- **Pv**: if no down payment is made, the current cash value is 0, if you use an initial capital, for example of initial deposit of €5,000, you must enter this value as a **negative value** again.
- **Fv** for the future final value. Select the cell with the final value of €10,000, and type = 1, as the payment is made at the beginning of the month.

Small Variant:

➢ Perform the above calculation, but in another row with the **initial capital** of €1,000. So change PMT again or manually in the formula: =PMT (B4/12; B5*12; -1000; B6;1).

12.2 Determining the Saving Rates

Now the final amount that can be achieved with a certain amount of savings is to be determined. The **FV function** is available for this purpose.

➢ Enter the required values on a new sheet.

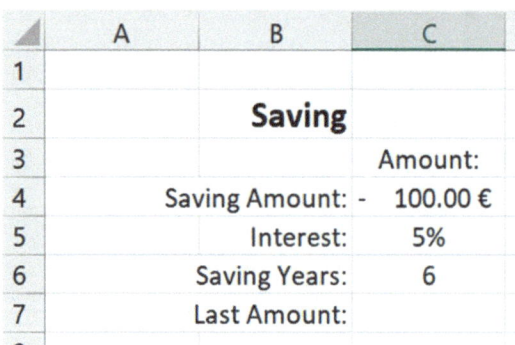

➢ Use the function wizard to access the **FV** function in the next line.

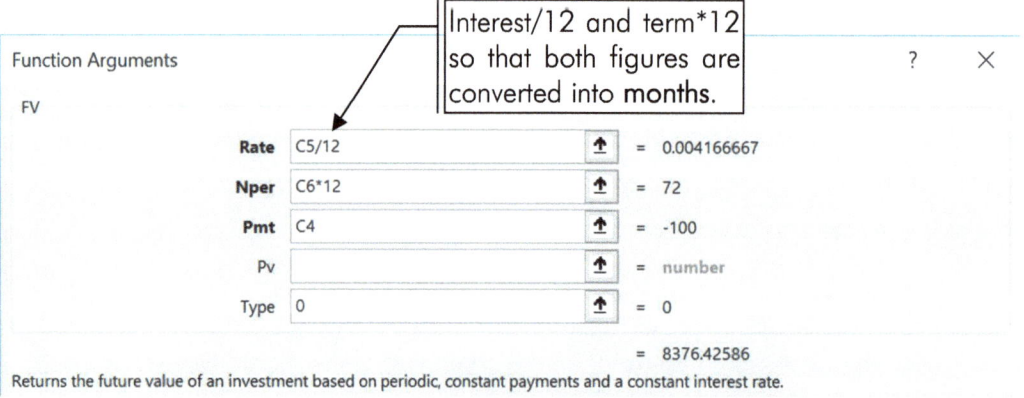

Interest/12 and term*12 so that both figures are converted into **months**.

Returns the future value of an investment based on periodic, constant payments and a constant interest rate.

➢ Since we click on the cells instead of entering the values, you can change the values and simulate other conditions. That's also good for control. To check the formula, choose a term of one year and 10 years.

12.3 Saving by Handwork

It makes sense not only to calculate the savings development manually for checking purposes but also, for example, because individual special payments with date could be entered and interest rate fluctuations could be taken into consideration.

A table could be set up like this:

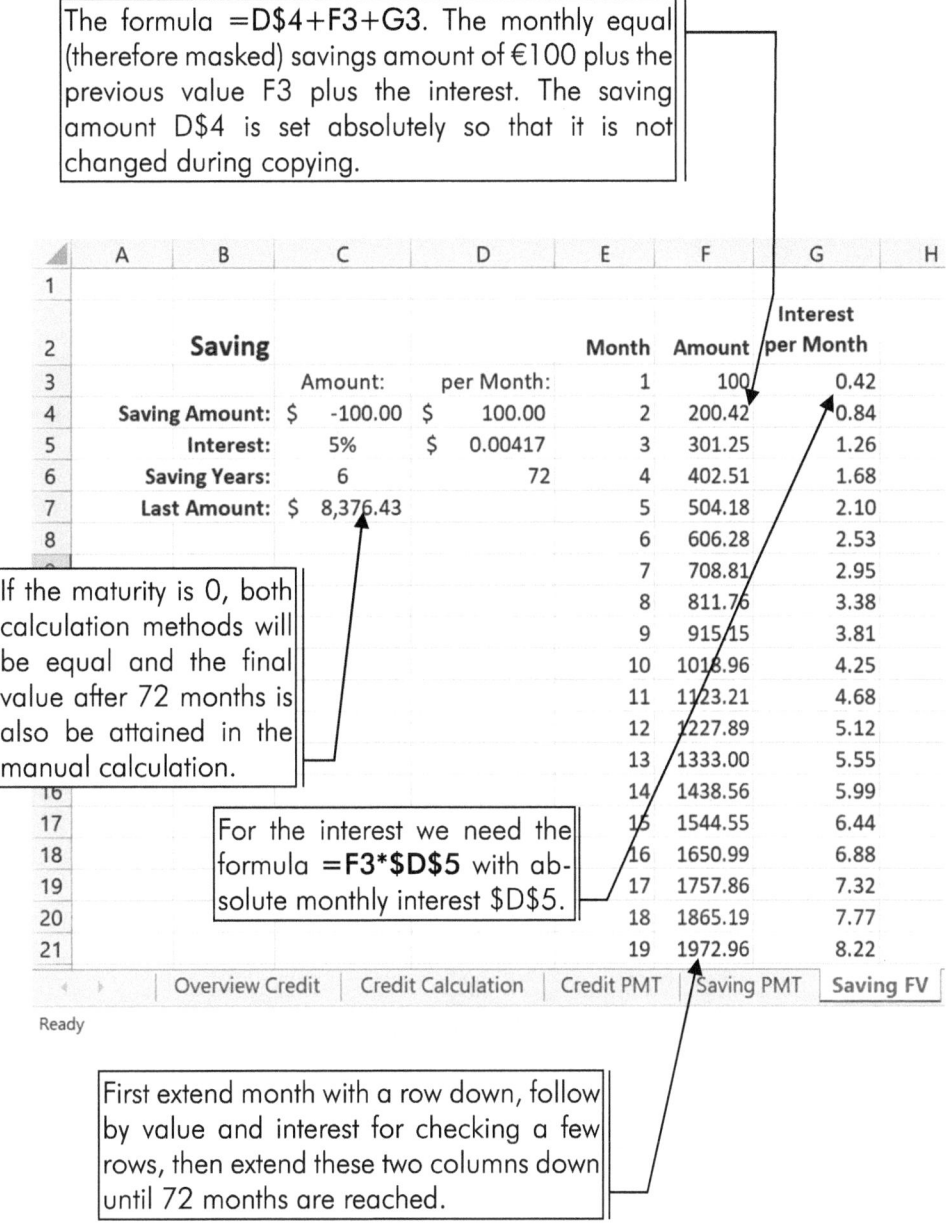

The formula =D$4+F3+G3. The monthly equal (therefore masked) savings amount of €100 plus the previous value F3 plus the interest. The saving amount D$4 is set absolutely so that it is not changed during copying.

If the maturity is 0, both calculation methods will be equal and the final value after 72 months is also be attained in the manual calculation.

For the interest we need the formula =F3*$D$5 with absolute monthly interest $D$5.

First extend month with a row down, follow by value and interest for checking a few rows, then extend these two columns down until 72 months are reached.

For consecutive line numbering, use the Row function first; if all three columns contain several rows, they can also be extended together with the mouse.

The manual calculation results in 8.376.43 Euro, which corresponds to the formula FV with the due date 0, i.e. payment of interest at the end of the month. Interest at the beginning of the month would have to be applied to a loan.

12.4 Help for the Formulas

In the function wizard, you will find "**Help for this Function**" for each function below. In the help menu that appears, the formulas are described in detail with the LIA function as an example.

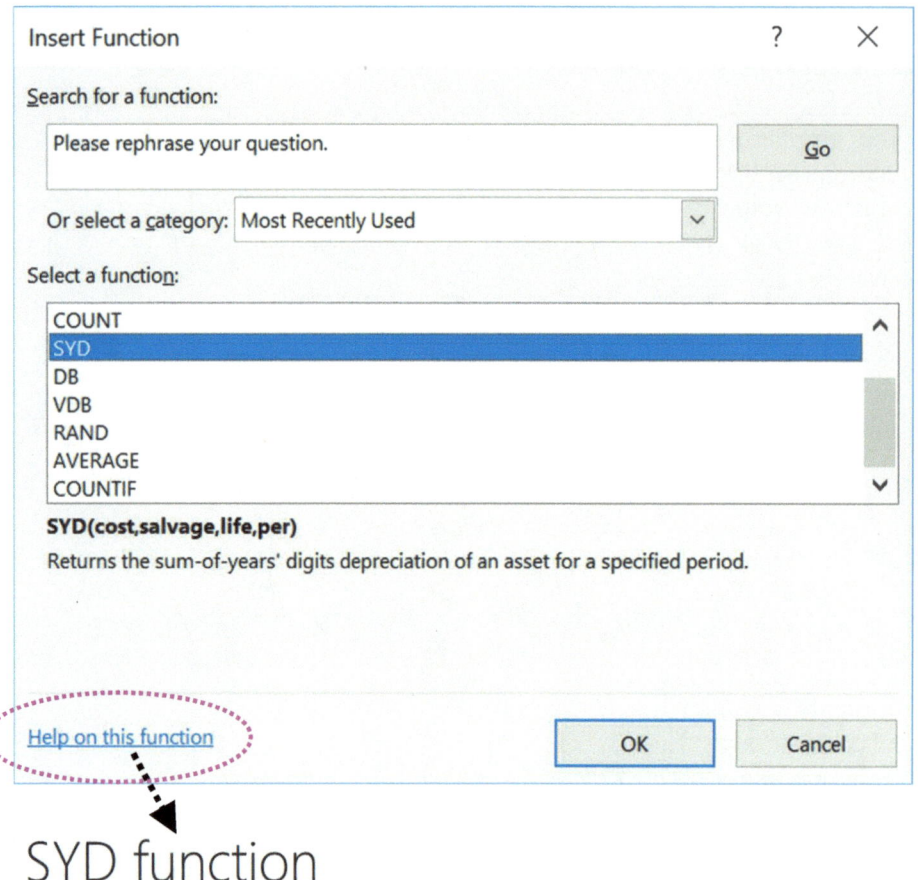

SYD function

Applies To: Excel for Office 365, Excel for Office 365 for Mac, Excel 2016, Excel 2013, More...

This article describes the formula syntax and usage of the **SYD** function in Microsoft Excel.

Description

Returns the sum-of-years' digits depreciation of an asset for a specified period.

Syntax

SYD(cost, salvage, life, per)

The SYD function syntax has the following arguments:

- **Cost**   Required. The initial cost of the asset.

- **Salvage**   Required. The value at the end of the depreciation (sometimes called the salvage value of the asset).

- **Life**   Required. The number of periods over which the asset is depreciated (sometimes called the useful life of the asset).

- **Per**   Required. The period and must use the same units as life.

Part 4
Advanced Formatting

With colors, frames, graphics and style sheets for professional excel sheets

13. Hide, Draw

13.1 Hide

Finally, we **format** the credit or interest calculation attractively with a little expansion. The many lines of all unused cells disturb the overall picture. Please, Try the following:

> ➤ Select the **lines not needed** on the screen,
>
> ➤ then select white as **background color** with the paint bucket.
>
> ➤ Also, select the unused **columns** and format them in white.

Now the Header:

> ➤ Set the right mouse button row height to 28 for the header (not possible if the cell was opened by double-clicking).
>
> ➤ Select heading, right mouse button and format cells. Increase the **font size** to **20 pt**, set **vertical alignment** across both columns, text color, and frame.
>
> ➤ Enhance formatting with border lines and cell styles.
>
> ➤ Add the **blank lines** to divide the calculation into lucid blocks.

This is the way it could be:

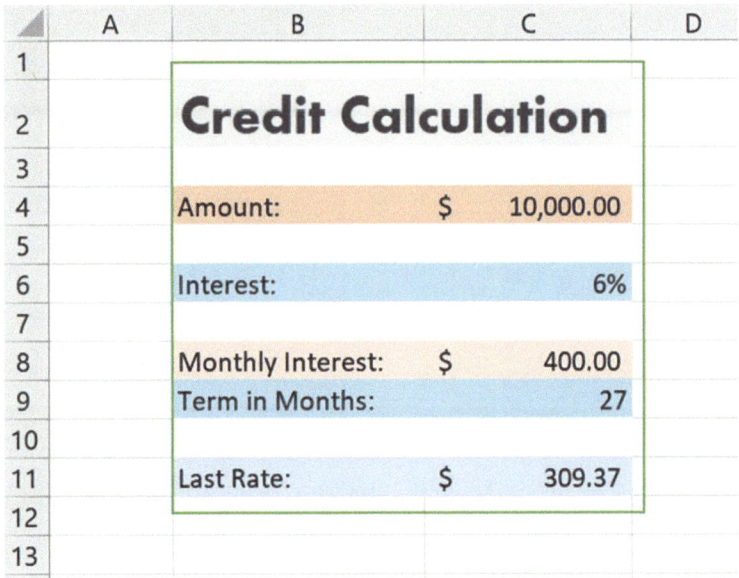

13.2 Drawing in Excel

The **Rectangle** can also be drawn using the Drawing Functions.

> Delete frame lines, then drag a **rectangle** over the table with the mouse button pressed on the **Insert** for shapes tab:

The Draw toolbar will automatically appear:

Disable the Filling for Shape Fill.

Text Box = Frame for Text Input

Select Preset or here with the small **extension arrow** to the menu for Fill, Line, and Font color.

Special lines, Arrows, labelling fields, etc. (with [Shift]-key Circle or Square)

> Draw a rectangle over the whole table and deselect its Fill color:
>   ↳ To do this, click on the Rectangle and
>   ↳ Select "No Fill" in the Toolbar for the Filling effect.

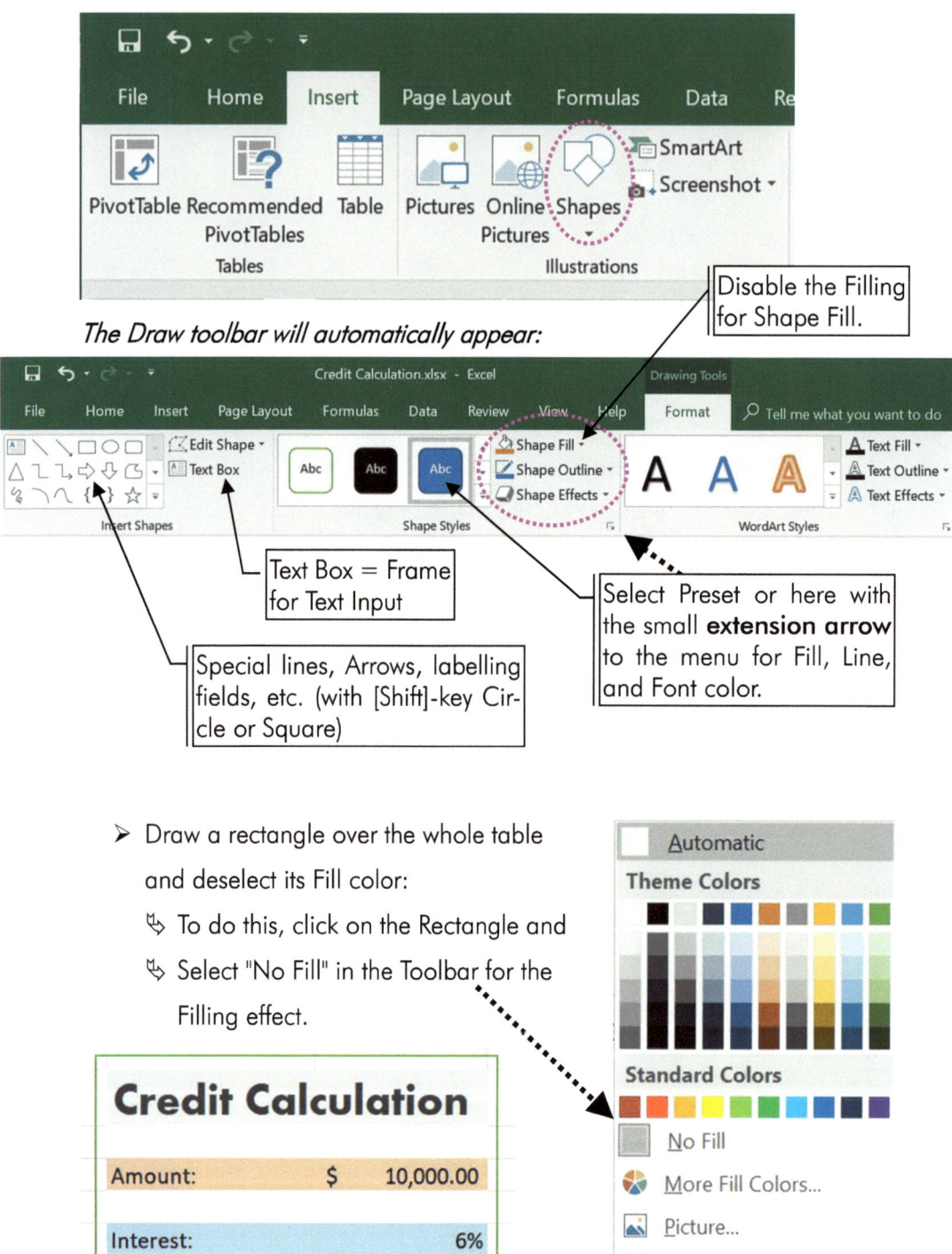

> **Deactivate** the toolbar: Simply click on another cell to return to the normal toolbar.

Other Formatting:

With the Shapes (formerly AutoShapes) you will find numerous ready-made graphic shapes, e.g. a Rectangle with rounded corners, an Octagon, various Arrows, Icons for Flowcharts, Stars, and Banners.

Rectangle with rounded shapes.

All auto shapes can be changed later:

- ♦ Rounded shapes go like this afterward:
    - ✋ Click on Rectangle,
    - ✋ then click **Drawing Tools** at the top of the program bar and then
    - ✋ **Edit Shape** to select the rounded rectangle.

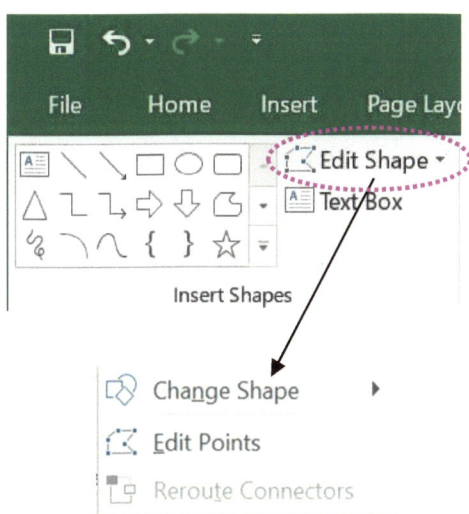

You can add Text to all Auto shapes:

- ♦ **Click on the shape** and simply start typing or **right-click** on the Auto shape and select "**Edit Text**".
- ♦ With all AutoShapes, you will find numerous setting options using the **right mouse button** and "**Format Shape**", for insatance, various fill patterns or color gradients.

Complete Exercise:

- ➢ **Rename** the Sheets appropriately: Credit, Calculation, Credit with PMT, Saving with PMT.
- ➢ **Print** the Spreadsheet. Use the printout to complete the table, as the result will vary depending on the printer.

13.3 Cell Styles

In addition to the templates for new tables, it is possible to assign preset formatting to existing tables.

So far, we have formatted tables manually in order to get to know all setting options. Excel can format standard tables independently.

If the tables have special features such as multiple Headers, you can still format them manually or edit the automatic formatting.

➢ Open the exercise **Car Depreciation** (see chapter 7.2).

The following formatting aids are provided by Excel:

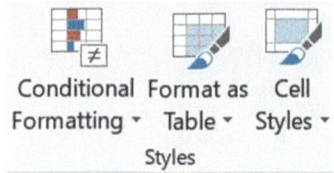

- ♦ **Format as Table**: here you can automatically format tables by assigning color schemes to them as before with Auto-Format. Procedure:

  ➢ First **select** the desired table follows by selection of a color scheme under "Format as Table".

  ✎ The following information window appears:

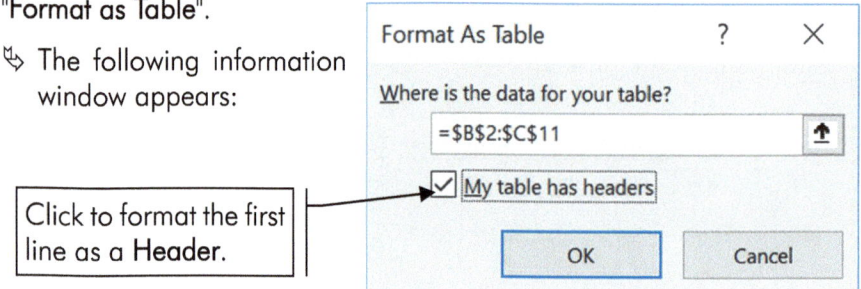

- ♦ **Cell styles**: here you will find different color combinations that can be assigned to previously selected cells.

  ✎ This means that separate areas can also be reformatted later, e.g. to adapt an automatically formatted table as required.

- ♦ **Conditional Formatting**: here you can specify that some cells with negative values are highlighted in color. Purpose: automatic selection of critical values.

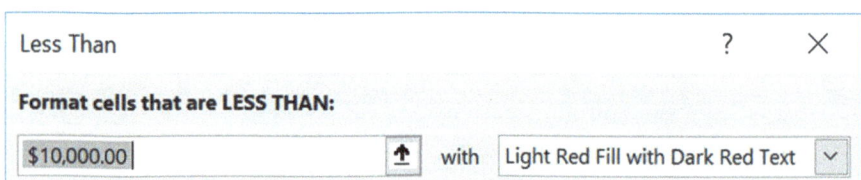

➢ Also, reformat **the Spreadsheets of the Credit calculation** with "Format as Table" or the cell format templates. You may try several different patterns.

> With **Undo,** you can remove formatting and try out different variants one after the other.

14. Styles in Excel

- Styles make work a lot easier, especially for professional use:
  - Instead of selecting and then setting each Header separately (font and size, text and background color, etc.), everything
  - is only set once in the **Styles** named Header.
  - For a new Table Header, simply switch to this format template and all the formatting is there!

> Here we will only create a simple exercise calculation. You can guess the great advantages of the styles when you consider a page-long calculation.

We will explore the format templates in a practical way using real estate financing:

- Create the following table by starting in the third row of column B:

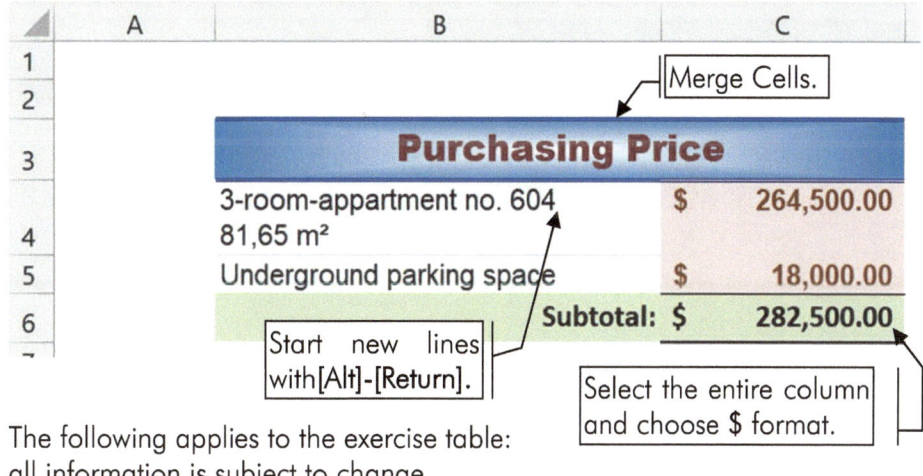

The following applies to the exercise table: all information is subject to change.

- Format the **heading Financial Requirements** shaded blue with red, strong font and borderline similar to the one shown above.

- Select the Rows and Columns that are not needed and hide them with the **White background color**.

14.1 A new Cell Style

➢ Click on **Financial Requirements** as the first main heading.

According window size cell styles are here to found:

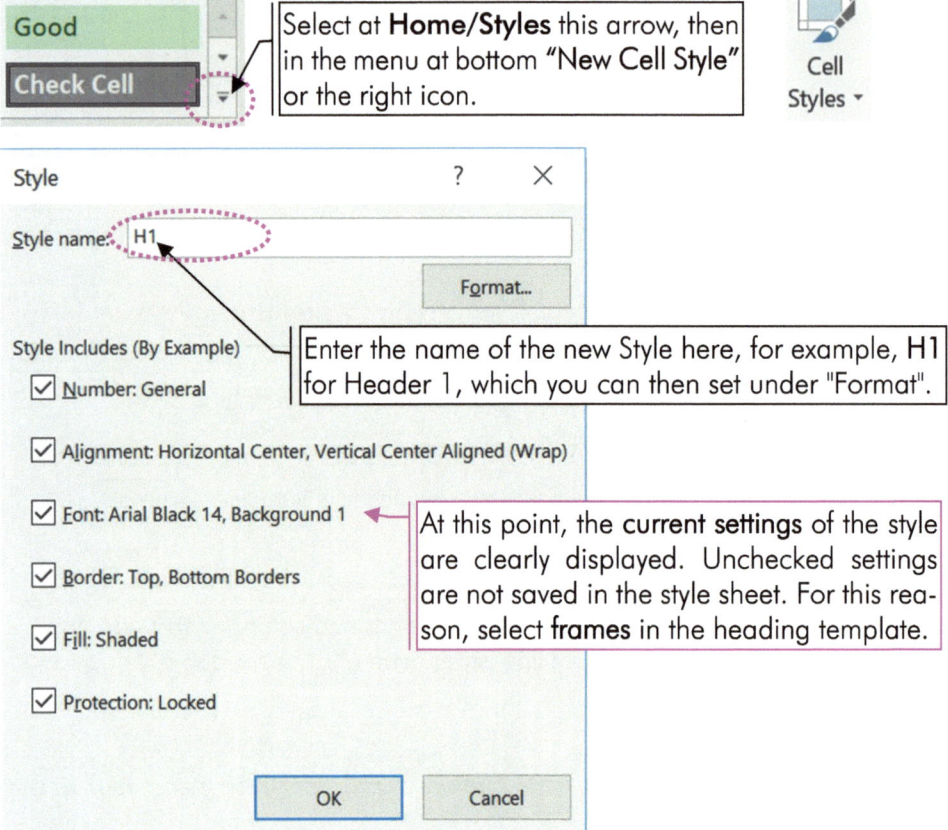

After OK, there is a new style H1 with the same settings as the Heading Financial Requirements. However, the style H1 must still be specified under the Heading Financial Requirements:

➢ Click on the Heading Financial Requirements, then select and assign the new H1 for **Cell Styles**.

✍ You can see that style sheets for **Headings** already exist in Excel, right-click on them and modify, then these can also be used as well.

14.2 Assign Styles

The Table continues after a blank line.

➢ Add the following text. In the figure, the single-color background on the Fill tab has been replaced by a **two-color fill effect "From the center"**:

Additional Charges		
Real estate transfer tax 3,5 %	$	9,887.50
Broker's commission 3 %	$	8,475.00
19% tax broker's commission	$	1,610.25
Notary commission 1,5%	$	4,237.50
Subtotal:	$	24,210.25

Move and Furniture		
Moving costs	$	3,000.00
Renovation costs	$	10,000.00
Furniture, kitchen, curtains....	$	15,000.00
Subtotal:	$	28,000.00

Additional purchase costs and "Relocation and Furnishing" are now also to be formatted as main headings. Now you can see the advantage of the Style Sheets because any complicated settings are no longer necessary.

> Click on the respective cells and use the **Cell Styles** button to select the H1 **Style**.

14.2.1 Setting or Modifying Styles

Styles can also be changed at any time:

> Open the **Cell Style Menu,** press the right mouse button on H1 and select **Modify**.

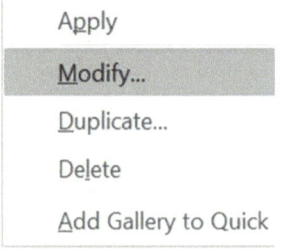

- In the menu that appears, you can create settings with the **Format...** button. Only that the changes now made apply to the Style.
- We could have also changed the Heading Financial Requirements manually and then saved it as a new format template U1.
- Also with the right mouse button, we can **Rename** or **Duplicate** styles such as the creation of another Heading U2 with similar settings and smaller font.

Configure the following:

> Bold **Font** + **Italic** and two dots **larger** than the rest of the Text
> and try the background color when filling the Fill Effect "from the center" with **light blue** and two dark blue including the thick **lines** at the top and bottom (tab frame).
> Then exit the menu with **OK**.

> You can reopen the style menu at any time and set the style differently. All texts to which this style is assigned are then automatically updated - please try it out, that is, choose a different Background Color.

♦ *You can easily access the menu with the keyboard shortcut [Alt]-t-v.*

14.2.2 Complete Exercise

The format templates cannot be set to merge cells; this must be done manually with the Icon to **merge cells**.

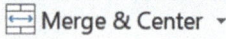

Now the exercise should look like this with the entered text formatted using styles:

For Formulas such as the land transfer tax C4*3.5%; Additional Formulas are used.

Purchasing Price

3-room-appartment no. 604 81,65 m²	$	264,500.00
Underground parking space	$	18,000.00
Subtotal:	$	282,500.00

Additional Charges

Real estate transfer tax 3,5 %	$	9,887.50
Broker's commission 3 %	$	8,475.00
19% tax broker's commission	$	1,610.25
Notary commission 1,5%	$	4,237.50
Subtotal:	$	24,210.25

Move and Furniture

Moving costs	$	3,000.00
Renovation costs	$	10,000.00
Furniture, kitchen, curtains….	$	15,000.00
Subtotal:	$	28,000.00

Credit Calculation *(Cell Style H1)*

Total investment	$	334,710.25
Own capital	$	60,000.00
$10,000 security charge	$	10,000.00
Total financial demand *(Cell Style H2)*	$	284,710.25

Cost of Financing

Rate of interest 5.2%		14,804.93 €
Back payment 1%		2,847.10 €
Subtotal:	$	17,652.04
Per month	$	1,471.00

Other Monthly Costs

Land tax	$	70.00
Additional costs	$	300.00
Renovation reserve	$	100.00
Subtotal:	$	470.00

Total Sum

Financial demand per month	$	1,941.00

14.2.3 Change Styles

Another new Stylesheet:

The sums should also be formatted uniformly. Here is the exercise based on the **subtotals** and **gross financial needs**, etc.

- ➢ Format the first Subheading similar to the figure,
- ➢ click and create a new Style H2.
- ➢ Then also assign this style H2 to the other Subheadings.

14.2.4 More about Styles

Both the Text and the Figures should be formatted with the **Heading 2 (H2)** style to ensure that the font and frame settings are consistent.

- ♦ The number format Accounting can already be defined in the style sheet.
- ♦ In this case, set the **alignment** to right-justified, which can also be done in the Style.
  - ✍ If the alignment is different, set the other column to a different position, such as right-aligned in the style and manually after assigning the style.
- ♦ Observe the existing styles which can also be Reformatted or Renamed and Used.
- ♦ Each style is based on the **Normal** Style and only reports what has been changed from Normal.

14.3 Advantages of Styles

If you subsequently change the style, all cells in this workbook to which this style has been assigned are automatically updated.

> Formatting is fast and easy for a very long Tables. This is the prerequisite for efficient setting of long Tables. Even if tables are spread across several spreadsheets, it is no longer a problem with styles to set them all uniformly.

An alternative to the format templates is the command "**Transfer format**" (see page 46) or **Format as a Table**.

- ♦ Even **longer Tables** can be formatted differently at any time without much effort (without format templates you would have to click on each heading again and change it individually)!
- ♦ A **uniform Appearance**: when formatting manually, a different value is occasionally set.

Part 5

Extended Applications

A test evaluation with graphical representation of the result, Trend, SVerweis and more

15. A Series of Experiments

Excel also provides some functions for scientific evaluations: Rounding, Highest or Smallest Value, Standard Deviation, etc.

Example: A **Tire Manufacturer** wants to test a new tread. For this purpose, six Braking Distances were determined at different speeds on a dry and straight Test Track.

Experiment Analysis Tire Profile A					
Speed	**30**	**50**	**60**	**70**	**100**
1	4,23	12,25	22,85	43,87	84,98
2	4,37	13,88	20,32	41,52	74,55
3	4,96	13,28	21,45	39,65	77,94
4	5,96	12,95	20,02	46,17	85,83
5	4,45	13,74	22,55	40,47	77,94
6	4,34	12,84	21,94	41,27	72,94

(Row label: **Test**)

15.1 Evaluation with Excel

With each test evaluation, the question of the respective **mean value** arises immediately especially since Excel automatically determines the largest and smallest **measured value**. If a value deviates very strongly from the mean value, it is often an indication of a measurement error occurring such as a value being read incorrectly.

Procedure:

- ♦ We will enter the **formulas** for a Number, Min., Max., Mean, and Standard Deviation once at Tempo 30 and then copy them into the other columns with the mouse.

You can find these formulas at formulas-fx in the category Statistical:

> **Number**,

> **Min or Max** (smallest or largest Value),

> **Median** and the **Standard Deviation STDEV.P**.

Note that Excel offers practically all calculation options, e.g. **Median** or **Geometric mean**, **Variance**, etc.

CHAPTER 15: A SERIES OF EXPERIMENTS   MS EXCEL 2016

This is how it's supposed to be:

Click on the cell and start the **function wizard** (*fx* or Formulas tab or with [Shift]-F3), select the desired formula and then enter the values with the mouse.

Speed	30	50	60	70	100
Test 1	4,23	12,25	22,85	43,87	84,98
Test 2	4,37	13,88	20,32	41,52	74,55
Test 3	4,96	13,28	21,45	39,65	77,94
Test 4	5,96	12,95	20,02	46,17	85,83
Test 5	4,45	13,74	22,55	40,47	77,94
Test 6	4,34	12,84	21,94	41,27	72,94
Quantity	6	6	6	6	6
Min	4,23	12,25	20,02	39,65	72,94
Max	5,96	13,88	22,85	46,17	85,83
Median	4,7183333	13,156666	21,521666	42,158333	79,03
Standard deviation	0,6020912	0,5543364	1,0568099	2,2121664	4,8507250

The preselection of Excel is to be corrected since the speed is also counted with the **number** and from Min upwards, the above values are no longer automatically recognized, but a formula and blank line precedes it:

Quantity:

either select right here and specify the correct cells without holding down the mouse button or

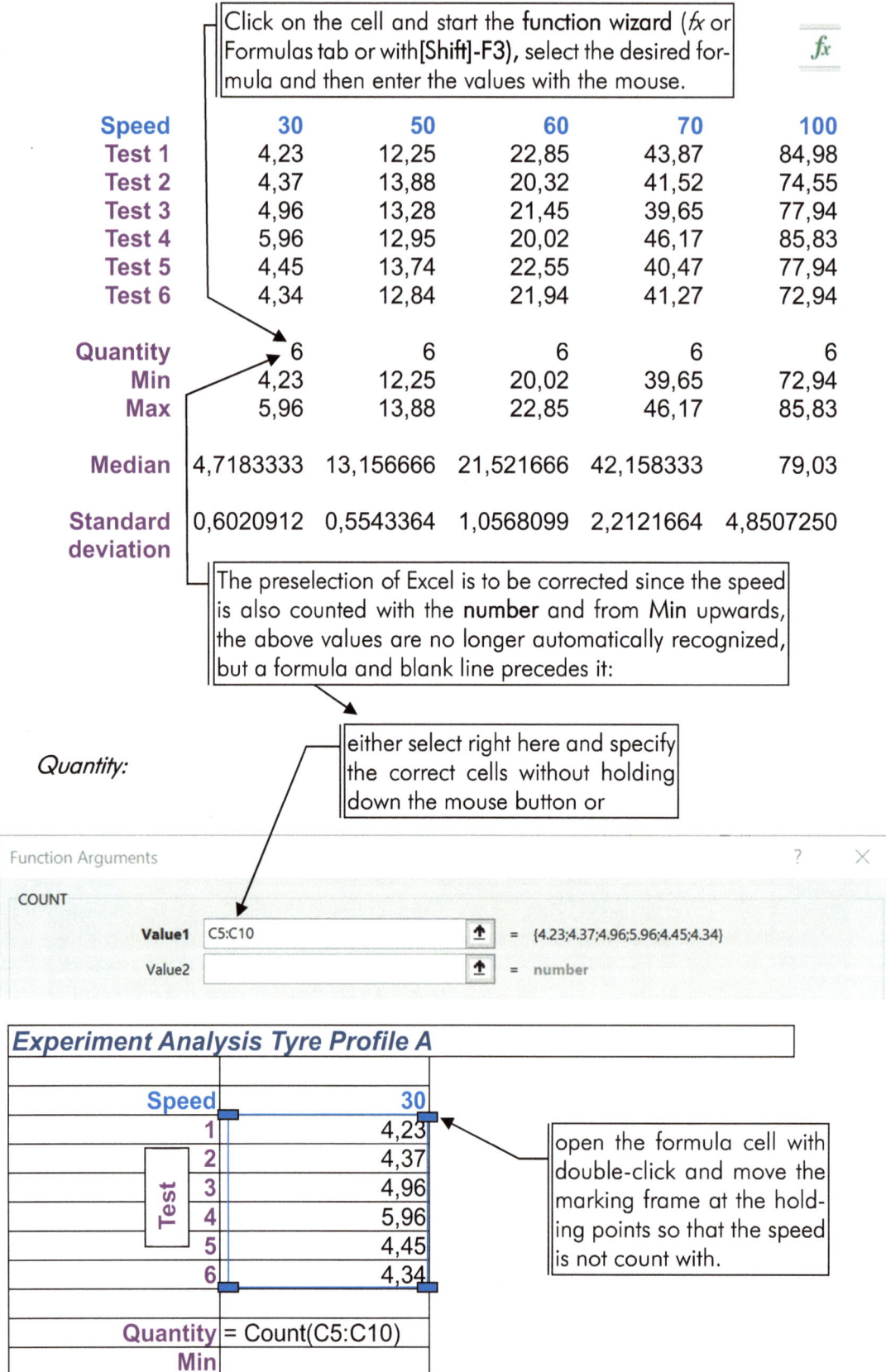

open the formula cell with double-click and move the marking frame at the holding points so that the speed is not count with.

> The same goes for the other formulas: Enter Min, Max, Median and Standard deviation (**STDEV.P**) and verify that the correct values are selected.

15.2 Rounding

The following problem occurs: the mean value and the standard deviation are displayed with too many decimal places. We have to round here.

> Highlight the first mean value 4.71833333 and press

> this Icon under **Start** several times to reduce the decimal places.

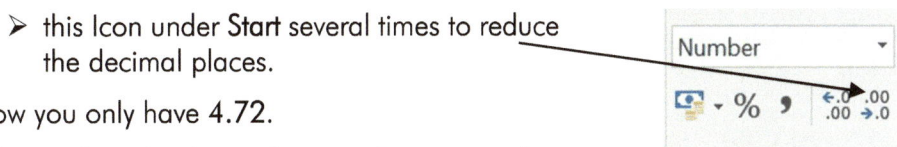

Now you only have 4.72.

Observe how Excel **rounds up or down** correctly.

> Repeat the same procedure for the Standard Deviation.

15.3 Copy Formulas

You can then copy the formulas to the right. You could select, copy and paste into the following cells, but it is even more efficient with the mouse.

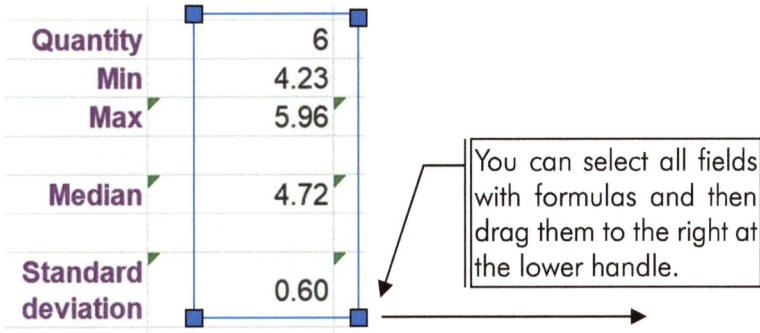

You can select all fields with formulas and then drag them to the right at the lower handle.

The function Edit/Fill/right is executed. Click on some cells to make sure that the values from the current column are always used for the calculation.

Quantity	6	6	6	6	6
Min	4.23	12.25	20.02	39.65	72.94
Max	5.96	13.88	22.85	46.17	85.83
Median	4.72	13.16	21.52	42.16	79.03
Standard deviation	0.60	0.55	1.06	2.21	4.85

> **Rename** this sheet in " Data ". Next exercise we add a new sheet for the chart.

15.4 Error messages in Excel

Since we have included three blank lines for the sake of clarity, a small **triangle** appears in Excel that requires attention.

➤ This is a **Smart Tag** (the green Triangle) and indicates that not all adjacent values are included in the calculation, but this is on a purpose and can, therefore, be ignored.

✎ An exclamation mark appears when you click on this Triangle.

✎ By clicking (wait until the arrow to open the menu appears) on this exclamation point, you can read more about the error message or

✎ **ignore** this **error**, which in this case, since the correct values for the formulas were selected manually is the best solution.

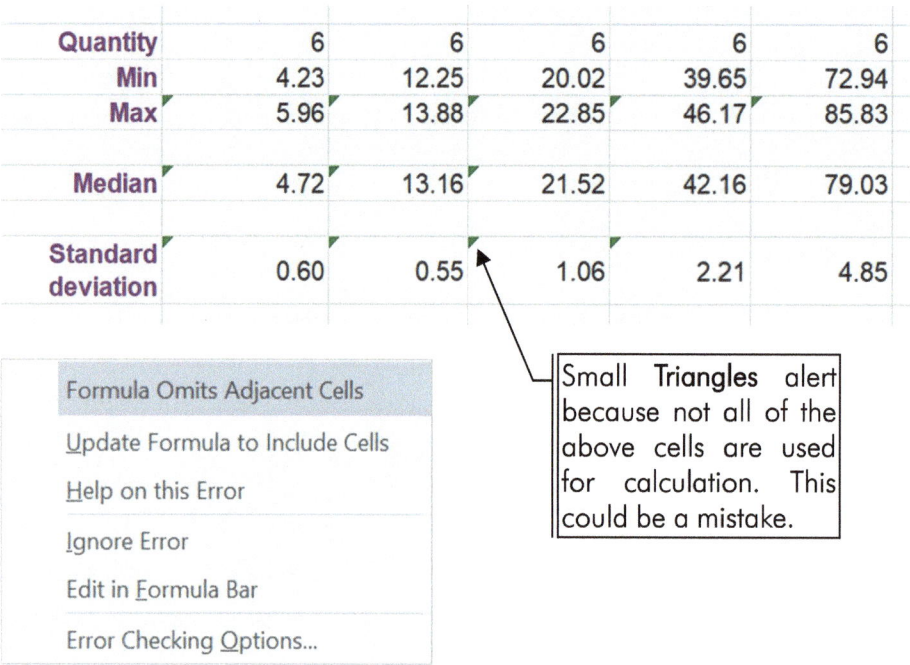

Small Triangles alert because not all of the above cells are used for calculation. This could be a mistake.

Hide all Error Messages:

➤ Start **error checking** on the **Formulas** tab.
➤ In this case, select **Ignore Error**:

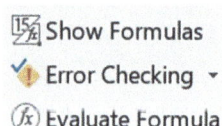

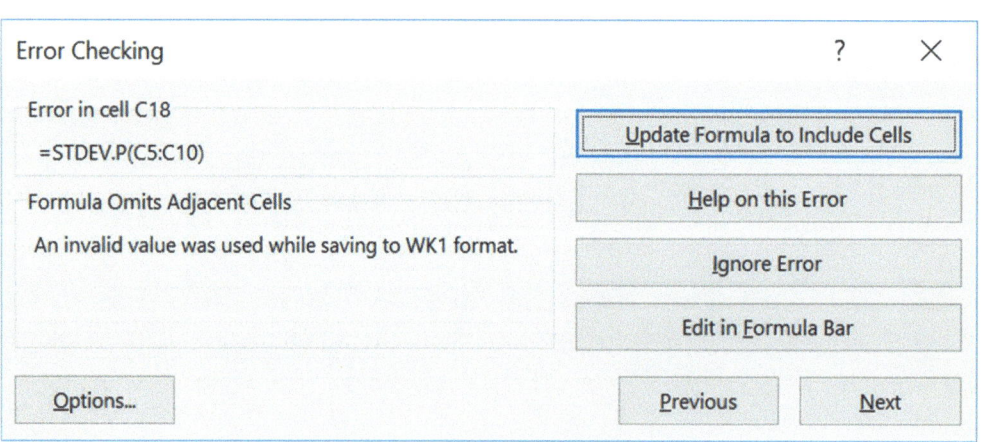

16. Create a Chart

In Excel, we can create **Charts** from data. This allows a series of measurements to be visualized and data to be presented, that is, at a meeting or presentation (prime examples: increase in turnover of a company or the sales figures of the branches).

We stick to our series of experiments:

> On the **Insert** tab, you will find several diagram types to choose from.

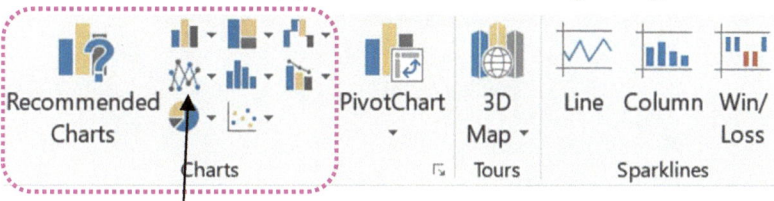

> The **line scheme** is ideal for this test evaluation. Select the line with data points and move the diagram area that appears so that you can see the data - This means you have also clicked on the diagram so that the symbols appear.

> Click on the Icon see left margin and select the experimental values without the **Headings**.

The diagram is created instantly:

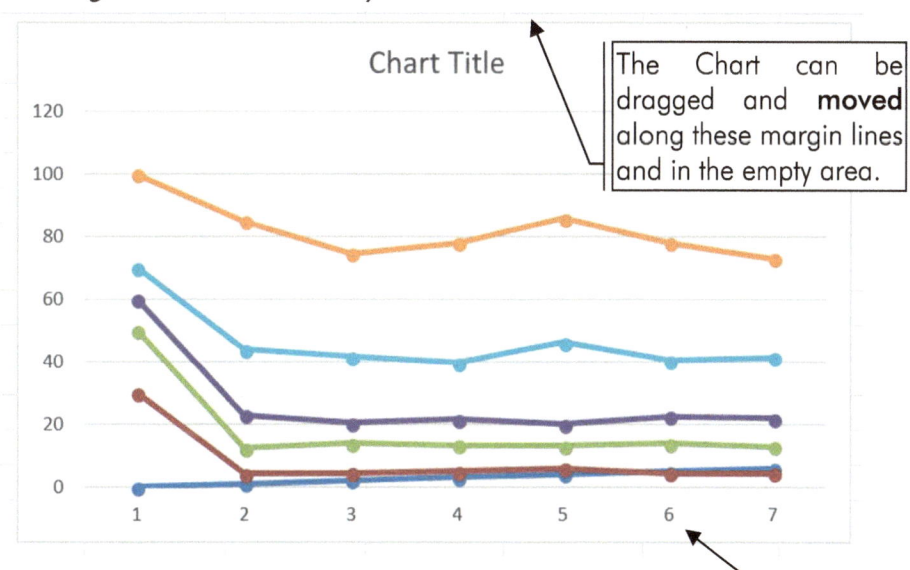

It can be seen that the Chart has not yet been set correctly. The speed should be displayed on this axis upwards the braking distance.

The Setting menu:

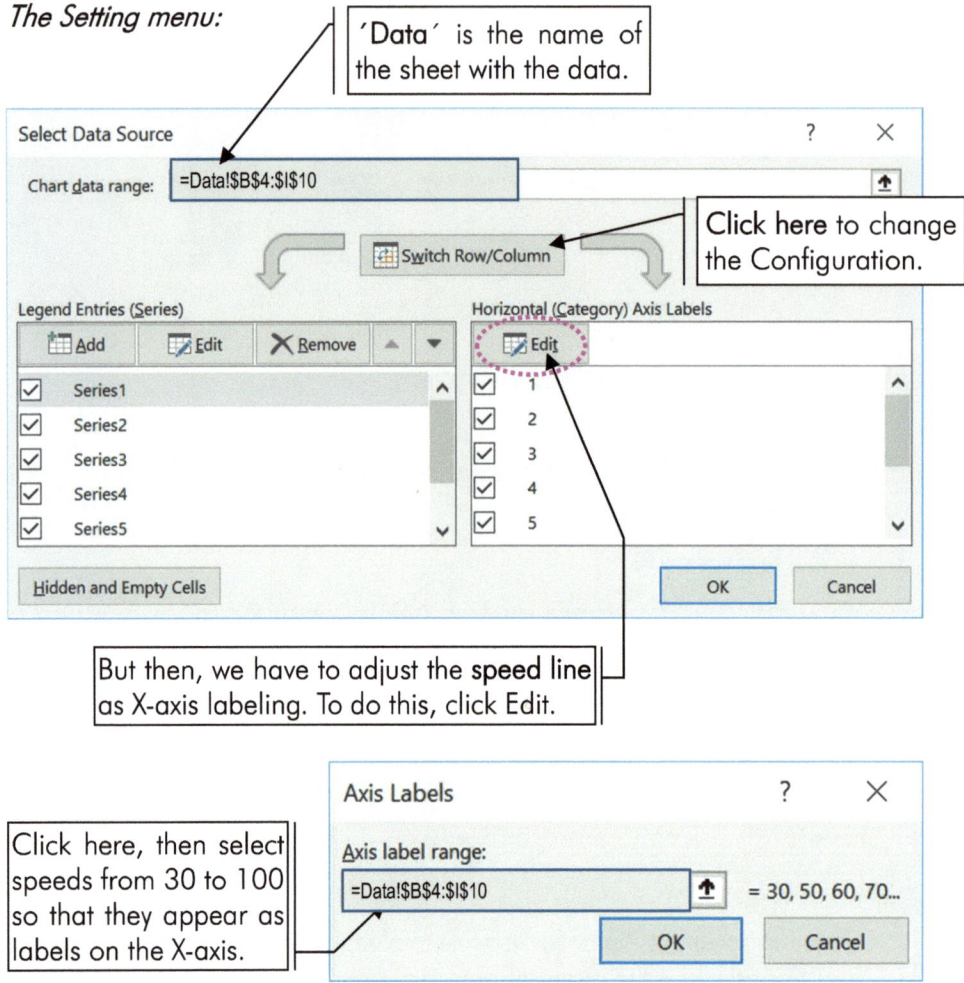

Now the arrangement is correct, but the axis labels are still missing:

> ➤ Select an additional **axis title** and a **key below** for the +.
> ➤ Click on the appearing axis titles and overwrite them horizontally with **speed** and upwards with **Braking Distance**.

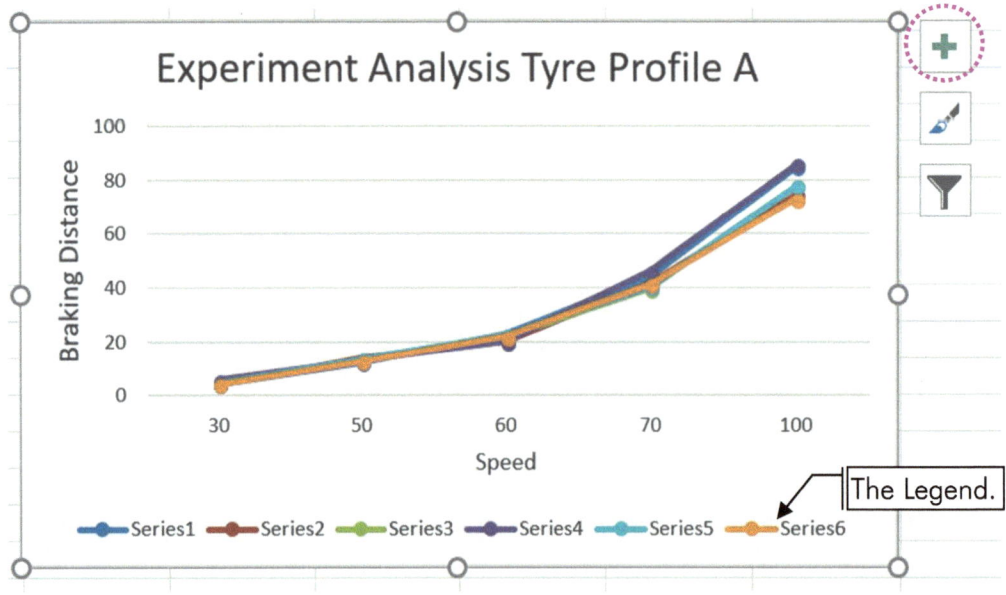

The values of the Y-axis are not yet optimal:

We only want the range from 0 to 90m instead of 100m as axis labeling, which can be set manually.

> Press the right mouse button on the Y-axis and select **Format Axis** in the drop-down menu.

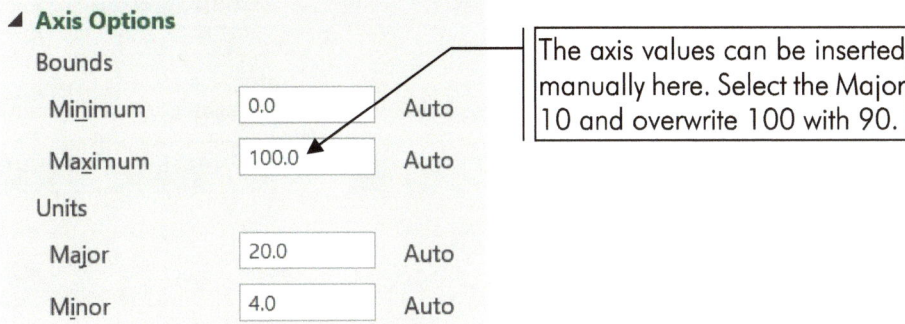

The axis values can be inserted manually here. Select the Major 10 and overwrite 100 with 90.

Change Chart Type

> If you have selected the "**stacked...**" Chart Yype, the Lines, Columns, etc. are displayed one after the other, i.e. the next y value + the y value of the previous measurement series.

> Try different display formats including stacked ones for the "**Change Chart Type**" Icon.

16.1 As A New Sheet

Since the lines are very close to each other, we should enlarge the chart so that everything is clearly visible. To have enough space for this, we move the chart to a new, separate spreadsheet.

> Select Chart and **cut** ([Ctrl]-X) and **paste** a new sheet.

> Then grasp at the corner and enlarge until the lines become clearly visible.

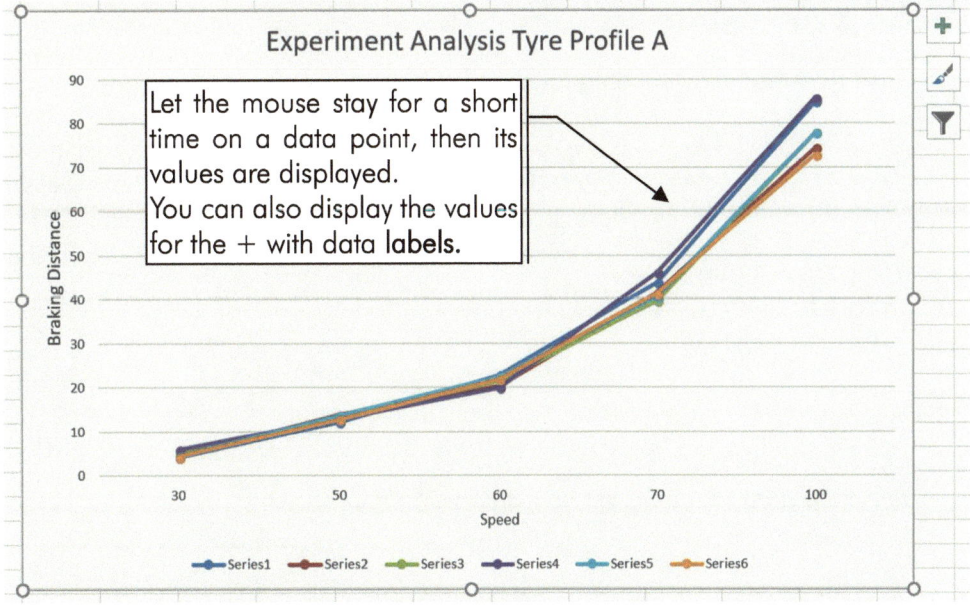

Let the mouse stay for a short time on a data point, then its values are displayed.
You can also display the values for the + with data **labels**.

> Rename the first sheet "**Table 1**" to "**Data**", the second with the chart to "**Chart**" and delete the third blank Sheet.

16.2 Overview of Chart Functions

A Chart can be changed in various ways.

Either with the Chart toolbar (click on the chart, then select Chart Tools above):

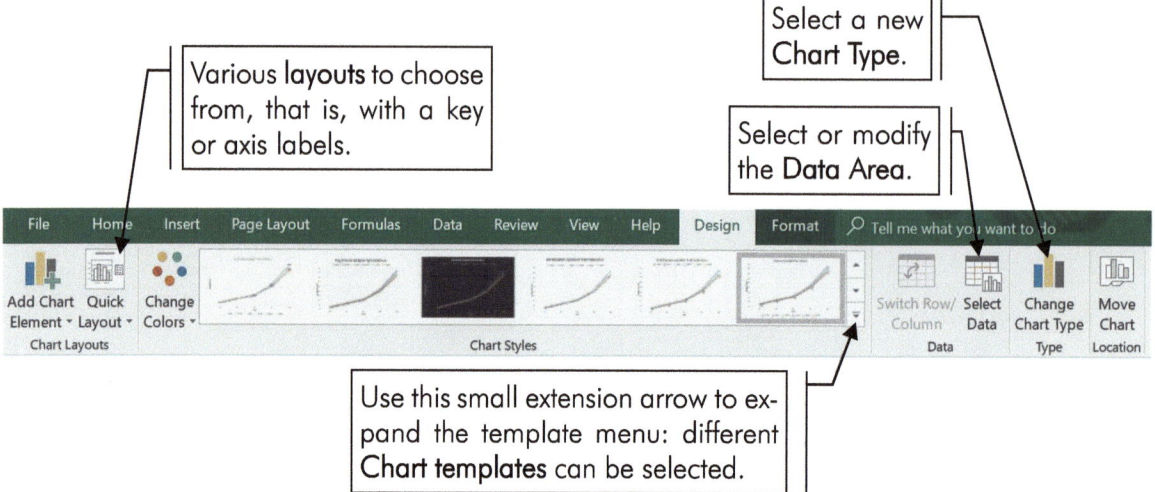

or with the commands at the top of the menu or with the right mouse button:

- **Right-click** on the Chart and appropriate commands appear to format the Chart. It is important on which element you press the right mouse button because the selected commands will be displayed, that is, you can
  - **change chart type** to another chart form or
  - choose a background color for **formatting the Drawing Area**.
- **Labels** can be clicked and deleted, formatted or changed.

16.3 Add or delete Values

➢ Add the following data for speed 130 and 200:

130	200
150.57	342.43
145.99	355.28
177.45	323.23
154.79	366.97
170.84	347.32
180.38	381.95

Now, these new values should also be included in the Chart. This can be done with the function "**Select data**" (icon at the top or with the right mouse button). This command is only visible if you have selected the Chart.

Select the data including the new data with the mouse:

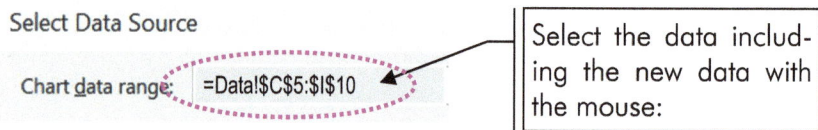

In addition, the manually entered scale range of the Y-axis must now be extended.

> Press the right mouse button on the Y-axis and select **Format Axis** from the drop-down menu, then expand the axis range from 0 to 90 to 0 to 400 and Major 20 or expand to Auto again.

It is even easier if the Chart is on the same Spreadsheet as the data.

> When you click on the **Chart**, a blue marking frame appears that indicates which data is used for the Chart:

Experiment Analysis Tyre Profile A

	Speed	30	50	60	70	100	130	200
	1	4.23	12.25	22.85	43.87	84.98	150.57	342.43
	2	4.37	13.88	20.32	41.52	74.55	145.99	355.28
Test	3	4.96	13.28	21.45	39.65	77.94	177.45	323.23
	4	5.96	12.95	20.02	46.17	85.83	154.79	366.97
	5	4.45	13.74	22.55	40.47	77.94	170.84	347.32
	6	4.34	12.84	21.94	41.27	72.94	180.38	381.95

At these points, you can drag the two **frame** columns further up to 200 with the mouse. The new data is automatically inserted in the Charts. You can also **remove data** by reducing the size of the frame.

The marking frame only appears if the chart is on the same spreadsheet as the data!

> Note: The values are similar to actual measured values, which is explained by the following physical background: double speed means four times the energy, i.e. four times the braking distance.

16.4 Final Exercise

Revenues are to be displayed graphically by Cities:

	San Francisco	New York	Los Angeles
2016	$ 1,245,000.00	$ 2,657,885.00	$ 2,146,443.00
2017	$ 2,564,546.00	$ 2,146,455.00	$ 1,944,355.00
2018	$ 3,165,547.00	$ 2,254,454.00	$ 1,745,464.00

Perform the following:

- Calculate the **highest value** of all three stores, as well as the lowest amount: Max, Min (imagine a page-long list where these values can no longer be easily recognized).
- **Format** the table appropriately (Format as Table).
- Display the values graphically in a **Chart** (see example). Switch to some other display forms to try them out.

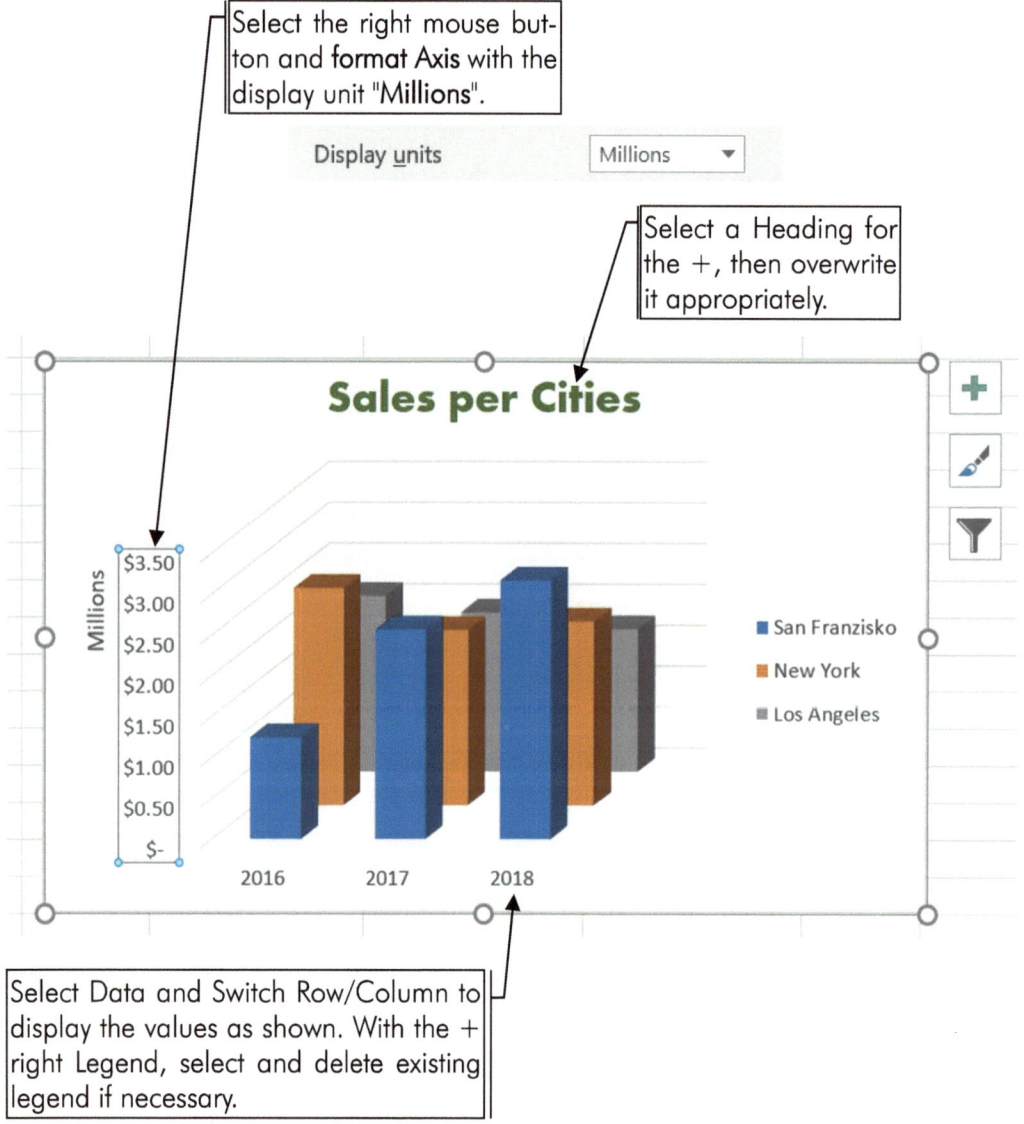

Select the right mouse button and **format Axis** with the display unit "**Millions**".

Select a Heading for the +, then overwrite it appropriately.

Select Data and Switch Row/Column to display the values as shown. With the + right Legend, select and delete existing legend if necessary.

17. Further Exercises

Finally, some exercises to deepen the material and to introduce some new formulas.

17.1 A Travel Expense Accounting

	A	B	C	D	E	F
1	Travel Expense Accounting from Mr. Mike Meiers					
2		from	01/06/2018		to	30/06/2018
3	19% VAT					
4	Date	Description	No.	Net	VAT 19%	Gross
5	01/06/2018	Taxi	852	$ 13.04	$ 2.48	$ 15.52
6	02/06/2018	Car service	853	$ 130.43	$ 24.78	$ 155.21
7	03/06/2018	Ikea	854	$ 100.00	$ 19.00	$ 119.00
8	04/06/2018	Railway ticket	855	$ 141.74	$ 26.93	$ 168.67
9						
10	06/06/2018	Restaurant	856	$ 17.22	$ 3.27	$ 20.49
11	07/06/2018	Taxi	857	$ 20.87	$ 3.97	$ 24.84
12	08/06/2018	Railway ticket	858	$ 233.04	$ 44.28	$ 277.32
13	09/06/2018	Fuel	859	$ 58.26	$ 11.07	$ 69.33
14	10/06/2018	Mobile phone	860	$ 318.62	$ 60.54	$ 379.16
15						
16	12/06/2018	Taxi	861	$ 8.61	$ 1.64	$ 10.25
17	13/06/2018	Pizza	862	$ 33.04	$ 6.28	$ 39.32
18	14/06/2018	Restaurant	863	$ 13.83	$ 2.63	$ 16.46
19	15/06/2018	Parking fee	864	$ 4.35	$ 0.83	$ 5.18
20	16/06/2018	Fuel	865	$ 47.83	$ 9.09	$ 56.92
21	17/06/2018	Mobile phone	866	$ 346.96	$ 65.92	$ 412.88
22			Sum:	$ 1,487.84	$ 282.69	$ 1,770.53
23	7% VAT					
24	Date	Description	No.	Net	VAT 19%	Gross
25	05/06/2018	Eating from supermarket		$ 35.51	$ 2.49	$ 38.00
26	11/06/2018	Dictionary		$ 378.50	$ 26.50	$ 405.00
27			Sum:	$ 478.50	$ 28.98	$ 442.99
28						
29					Sum total:	$ 2,213.52
30					VAT 7%:	$ 28.98
31					VAT 19%:	$ 282.69
32						

➢ Totals by Sum Icon (extend range), other Formulas by Pointing. Notes on the formulas follow on the next page.

Create this Travel Expense Accounting. Some hints:

- For **each month**, a new sheet can be used with the **annual accounts** following on another sheet, then a **new folder** for the next year is created.

- Most of the time you have **gross amounts** on the receipts resulting in the following formulas:
  - for VAT 19%: Amount/119*19,
  - net is then the **amount minus VAT** or amount 119*100.

- **Net amount** to be entered: **Net amount*19%** for the VAT.

- It becomes very clear with separate tables for **19% and 7% VAT** and a final totals are display.

17.2 Currency Table

There are also sufficient other currencies with the Euro. Not a problem with Excel. Firstly, an entry with some conversion rates which are of course not current[1], but are only for practice.

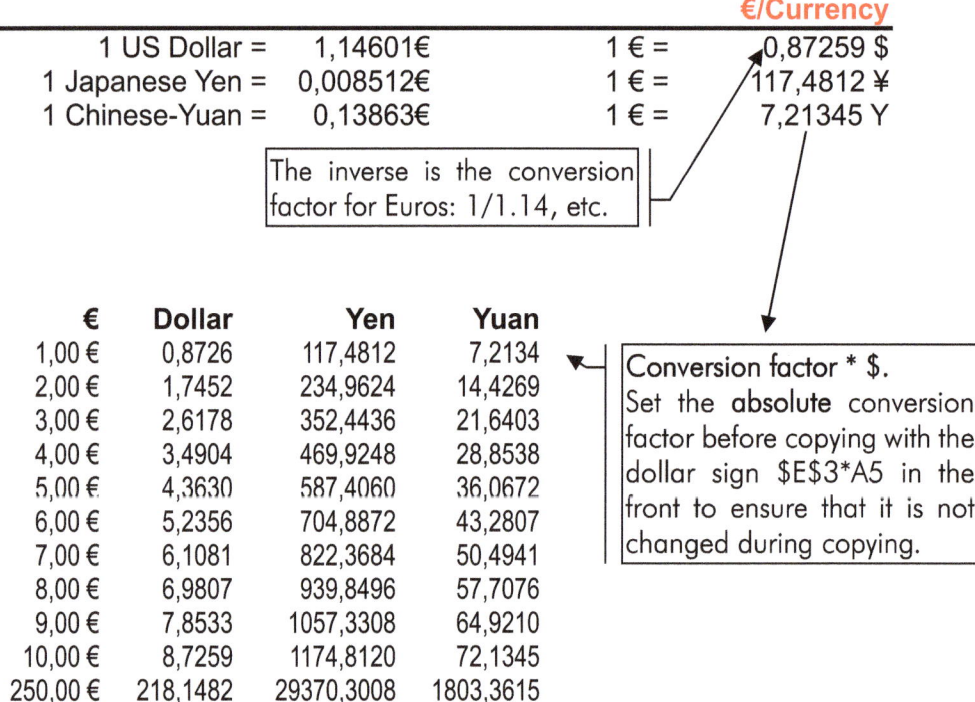

- Since **formulas** have been entered, you do not need to extend the list indefinitely, just **enter** the desired € amount in the left column and you will see the calculated value in the other currencies.

---

[1] Current currencies you find in the internet.

17.3 Score evaluation with VLOOKUP

An example from school. The Grades are to be calculated from the Scores obtained and the statistical distribution of the Grades is to be determined.

First, the Clef is defined (table from B4 to D11):

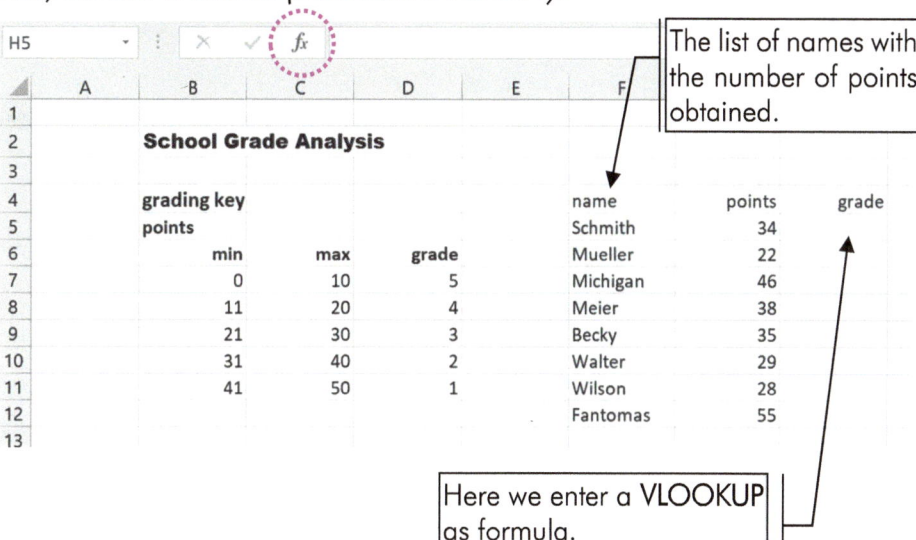

The list of names with the number of points obtained.

Here we enter a VLOOKUP as formula.

The **VLOOKUP** function can be found in the function wizard under "Lookup & Reference" and of course under "All"

The Formula Mask:

The values B7 to D11 must be masked with **$ characters** so that the formula can then be copied downwards without any changes.

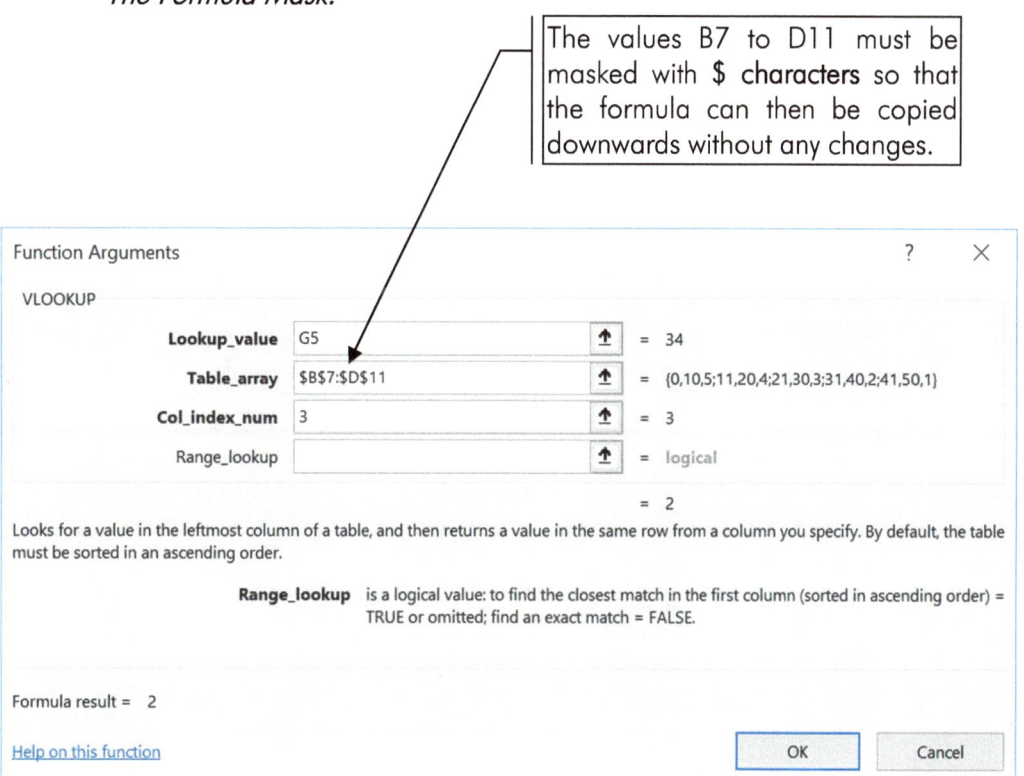

Description:

- G5 (=34 points with Schmidt) is **searched** for. This value is relatively changed during copying: G6, G7 etc.
- In the note matrix from **B7** to **D11**, the note for 34 points (=G5, Schmidt) should be found:
  - ✤ The first two columns are used to calculate where the value is to be assigned, and the third column is used to calculate the result.
  - ✤ To ensure that the same matrix is always used when copying the formula, mask with dollar signs in the formula:

    $B$7:$D$11 (=absolute remuneration).
- For Column-index, the column from which the value is taken is specified; enter the third column "Note", i.e. 3, here.

Grade distribution:

The Grade distribution is now to be calculated and displayed graphically. Add another table to the same spreadsheet:

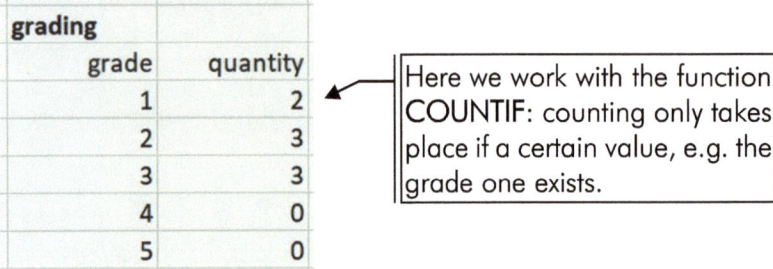

- We calculate the Frequency of a value with **COUNTIF** (statistically).
  - ✤ Select the Grade listing in the Name list (H5 to H12) in the **Range field** and set it to absolute with the **$ sign**,
- for **Search criterion**, select the first note 1 in the note distribution table shown on the left.
  - ✤ This value is relatively changed when the formula is copied so that the frequency of the Grade 2 is displayed in the specified matrix in the next field.

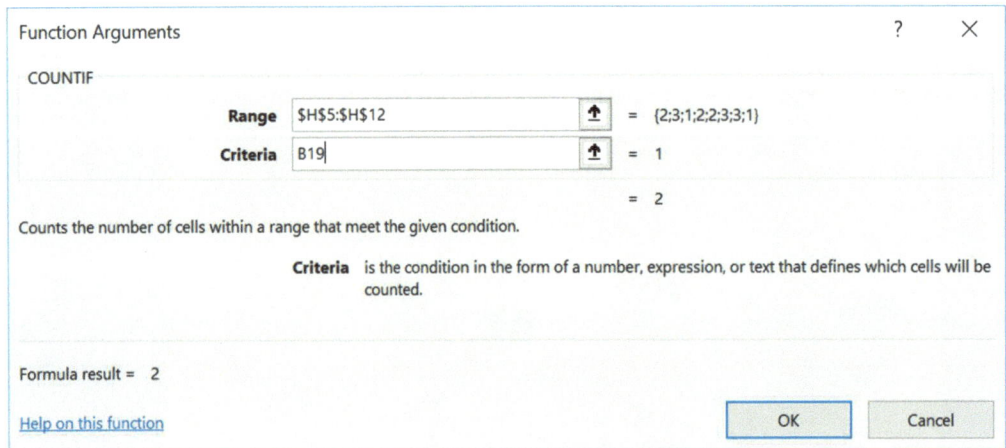

Graphical Evaluation:

That's no longer a problem for you. Create a Grade Chart as a Bar Chart. There's a little hint:

- Select only the **Frequency of the Grades**, not the Grade column itself, then select a Bar Chart when **inserting**.
- Select a **Quick Layout** with Title and Axis Labels, click and overwrite the labels.
- Click on the Y-axis, enter the right mouse button and **format** as Main Interval 1 for **axes**, Help Interval 0, since we only have integral Frequencies.
- Experiment with other forms of representation.

Of course, you can also calculate the **mean value**, which is 2.375 here.

You can find the Mean value in Statistics, then enter the Grades of the Name List as Values.

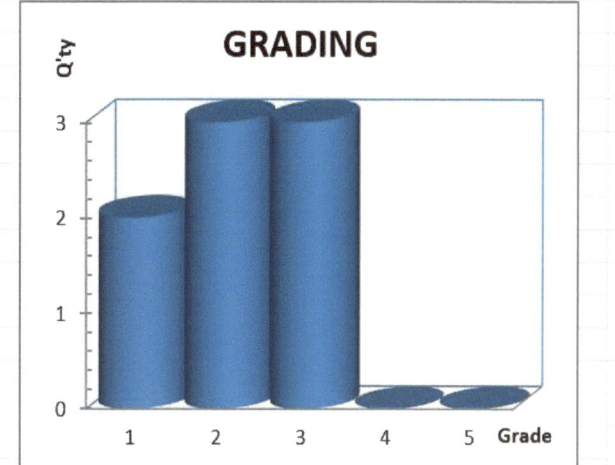

17.4 Monthly salaries with Bonuses

This is a case for **IF-Conditions**: *if salary exceeds the limit, then a Bonus*. That's the way it's gonna be:

Monthly Salaries with Bonus Payments					
Representative	Sales	Basic Salary	Bonus 1	Praise	Pay-Out
Mayer	28000	4000	1120	0	5120
Weller	19000	4000	0	0	4000
Stone	35000	7000	0	500	7500
Bush	22000	3600	880	0	4480

The values for Bonus, Praise, and Pay-out are to be calculated:

- The **following** condition (by logical) is inserted for **Bonus 1**:
  - **IF** B3 (Bonus) greater than (>) five times C3 (basic salary),
  - **then** 4 percent of turnover or 0%.

First, select the **Logic** category in the formula assistant, then start the "**If-Condition**" there and enter the values (B3 etc.) in the input mask by pointing and type the formula (>5*C3 and 4%*B3).

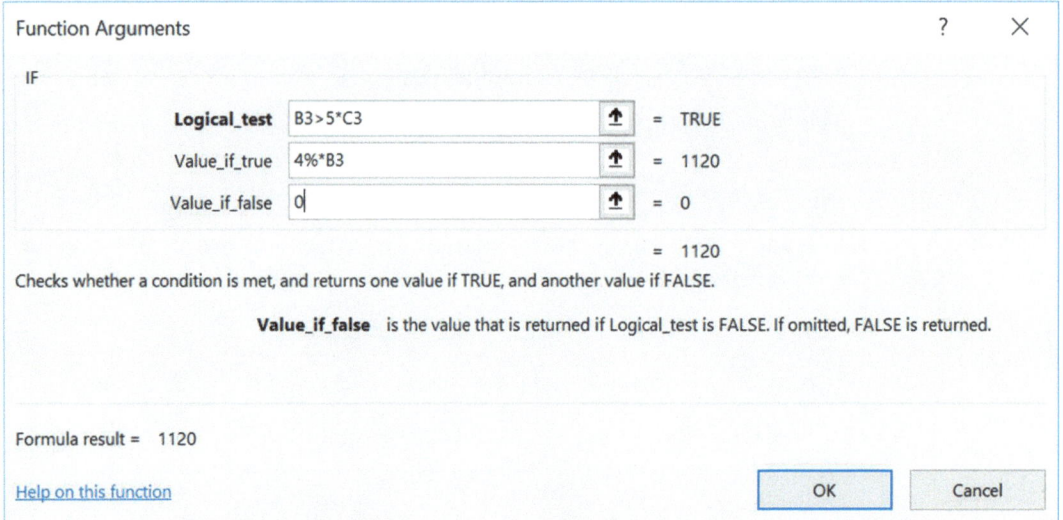

We have now entered a combined calculation and copied it into the following lines.

The formula for the Praise:

- IF B3 (Sales) is equal to (=) the **maximum value** in the Matrix with the Bonus (**$B$3: $B$6**),
- **then** add 500, otherwise 0 €.

In the formula, enter another formula MAX (just type). Set the matrix absolutely with $-characters before copying: ($B$3: $B$6).

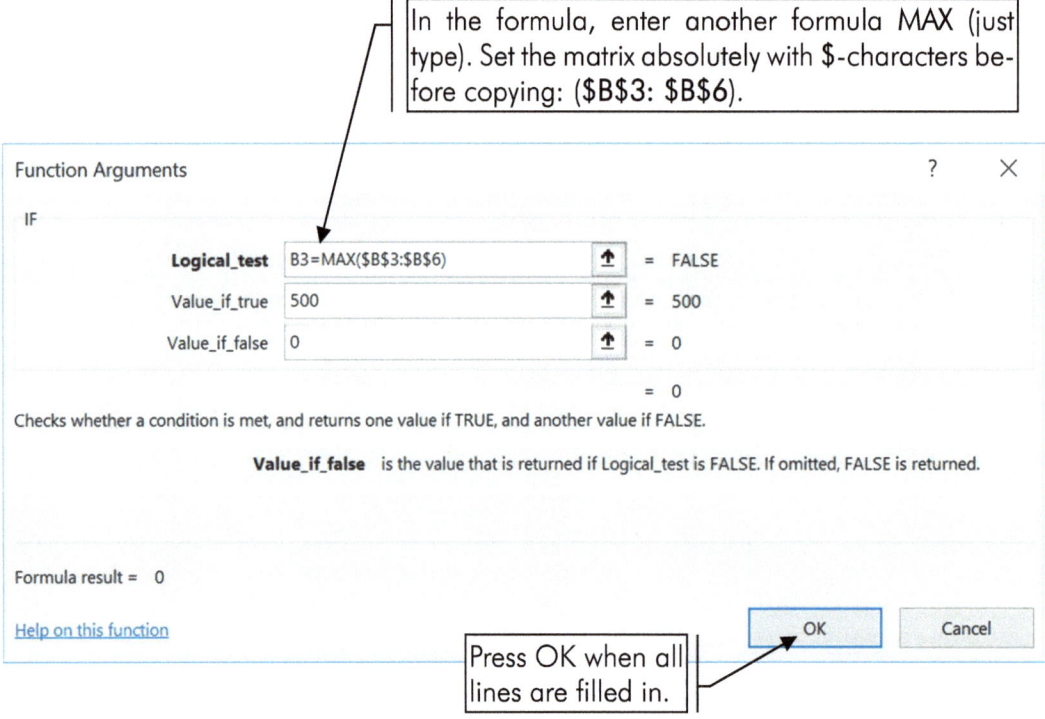

Press OK when all lines are filled in.

On **Pay-out** a simple sum: basic **Salary + Bonus + Praise**.

17.5 Logic

In Excel, we can output **TRUE** or **FALSE** and link it to the "**IF-Condition**", for instance, if red and blue it will be colorful. Other useful formulas are "**AND**" or "**OR**". This is explained using the example.

From an endlessly long list of computers with data, the following are to be filtered out for a Marketing campaign:

- Age above 18 **and**
- Income over €3,000 **or** rent over €1,000.

> To do this, we will content ourselves with a few **example values**, that is, enter these for **age, income and rent** similar to those shown below in a new table.

The output is TRUE or FALSE:

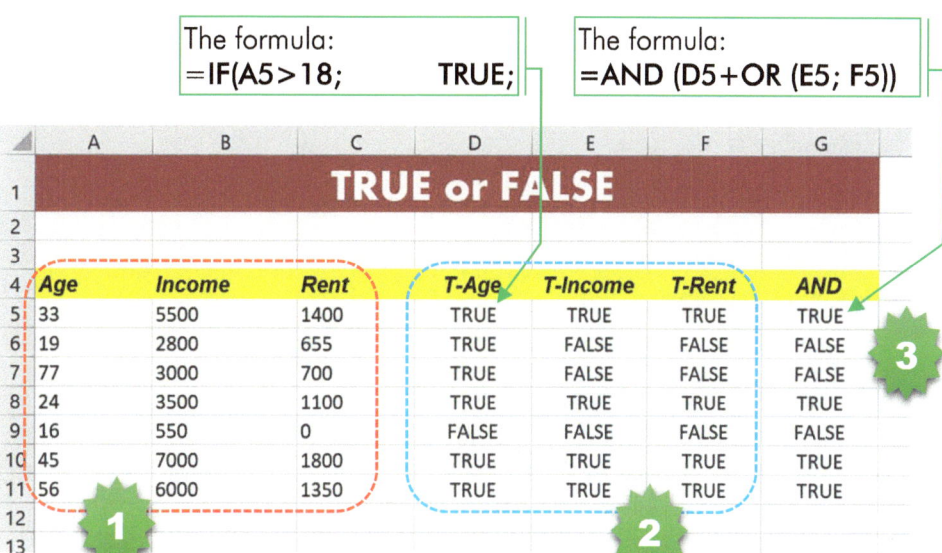

In order not to get a giant formula (also possible), we first determine these three **partial results** in a new column:

- T-Age: If(**Age**>18;TRUE;WRONG)
  ↳ i.e.: if you are over 18, enter TRUE, otherwise FALSE.
- T-Income: If(**Income**>3000;TRUE;FALSE)
- T-Rent: If(**Rent**>1000;TRUE;WRONG)

Now we already have "TRUE" or "FALSE" in the new columns, which we only have to link for the **final result**:

- **AND**Age;OR(Income; Rent)
  ↳ i.e.: Age > 18 **and** (income > 3000 **or** rent > 1000).

> In words: the formula returns "True" as a result if the age above 18 and either the income above 3000 or the rent above 1000.

The input menu for the "If formula" for T-Age:

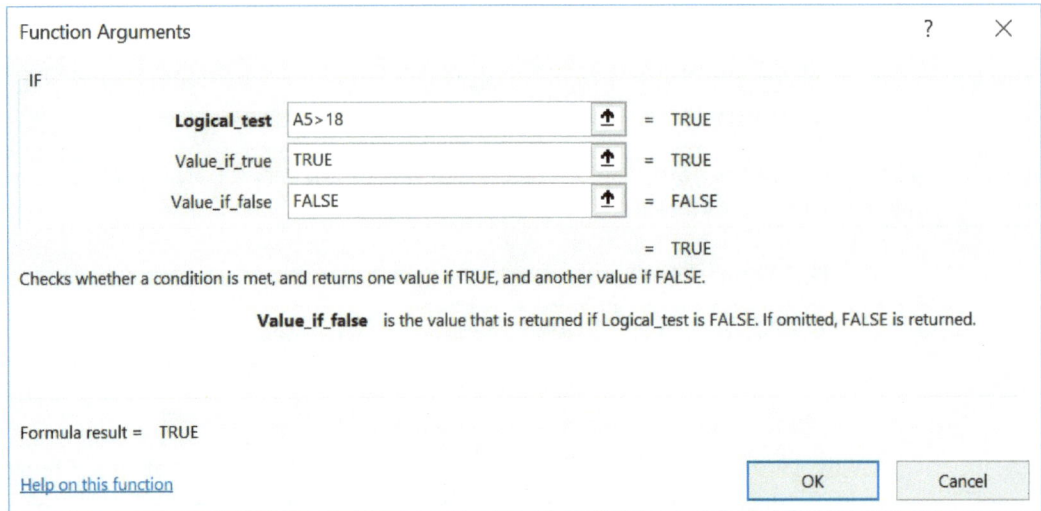

This results in the following formula:

=IF(A5>18; TRUE;FALSE)

- ✎ You could edit or type this formula by hand. The conditions must be in parentheses and separated by a semicolon.

➢ Then enter the If conditions for **T-Income (>3000) and T-Rent (>1000)**.

➢ and finally, evaluate them with the **AND-Formula**.

- ✎ AND can be found under Logic, too,

- ✎ then click on the first value at **T-Age**, continue to logical value 2 (see illustration) and enter an OR formula there: OR(E5;F5)

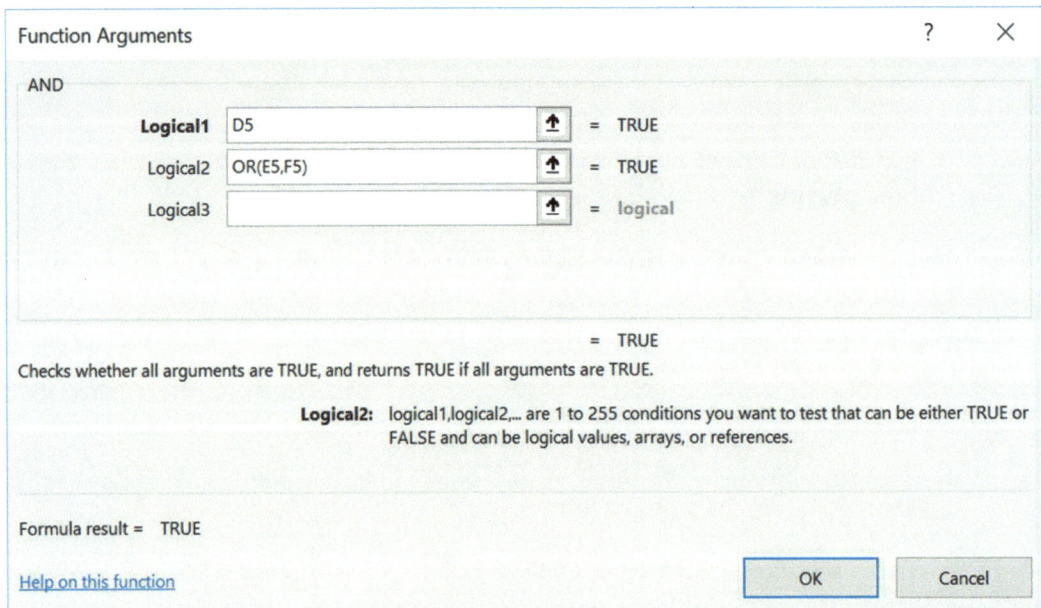

17.6 Trend Calculation

If continuously developing data is available, such as results of a test series, real estate prices or company profits; then, Excel can use the **Trend** function to show the expected development as a continuation of the initial values.

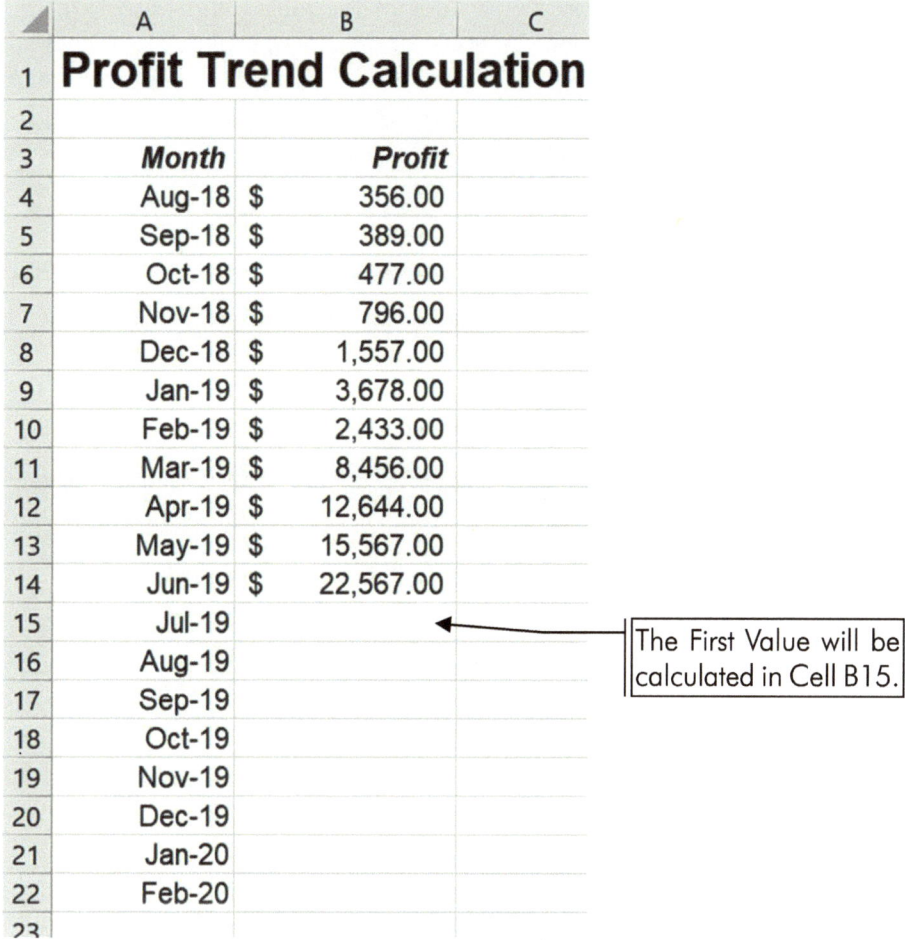

The First Value will be calculated in Cell B15.

> Click on cell B15 and select the function **Trend** in statistics, specify values by pointing and set Y and X values absolutely as preparation for copying:

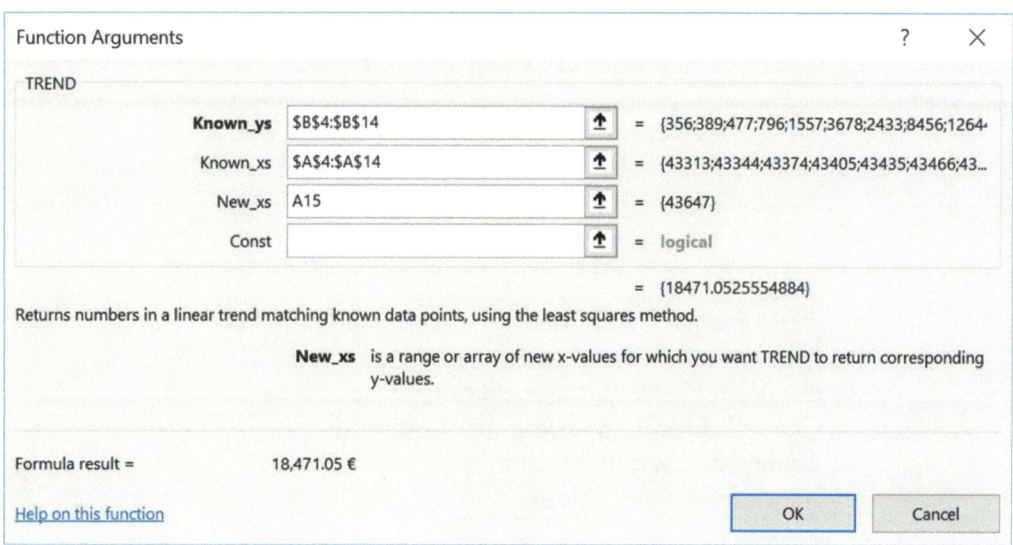

Explanation of the Values:

- The Y-values are the gains B4 to B14, the X-values are the months A4 to A14, the new X-value is the month of the first value to be estimated in A15.

- It is best to mask the existing values of the matrix immediately in the menu (=set with preceding $-character absolute), so that the calculated new values starting from B15 are not included in the further Trend calculation if we copy the formula downwards.

    =TREND($B$4:$B$14;$A$4:$A$14;A15)

> Then drag the first Trend-Result down to the other cells.

The first estimated value is unexpectedly lower than the last existing value since this last value had made a fairly large jump and includes Excel's tendency of all values.

The Trend Values are shown in the overview:

> Format the estimated trend values and annual figures with a different color.

> Create a **Chart** next to the data table that shows the development:

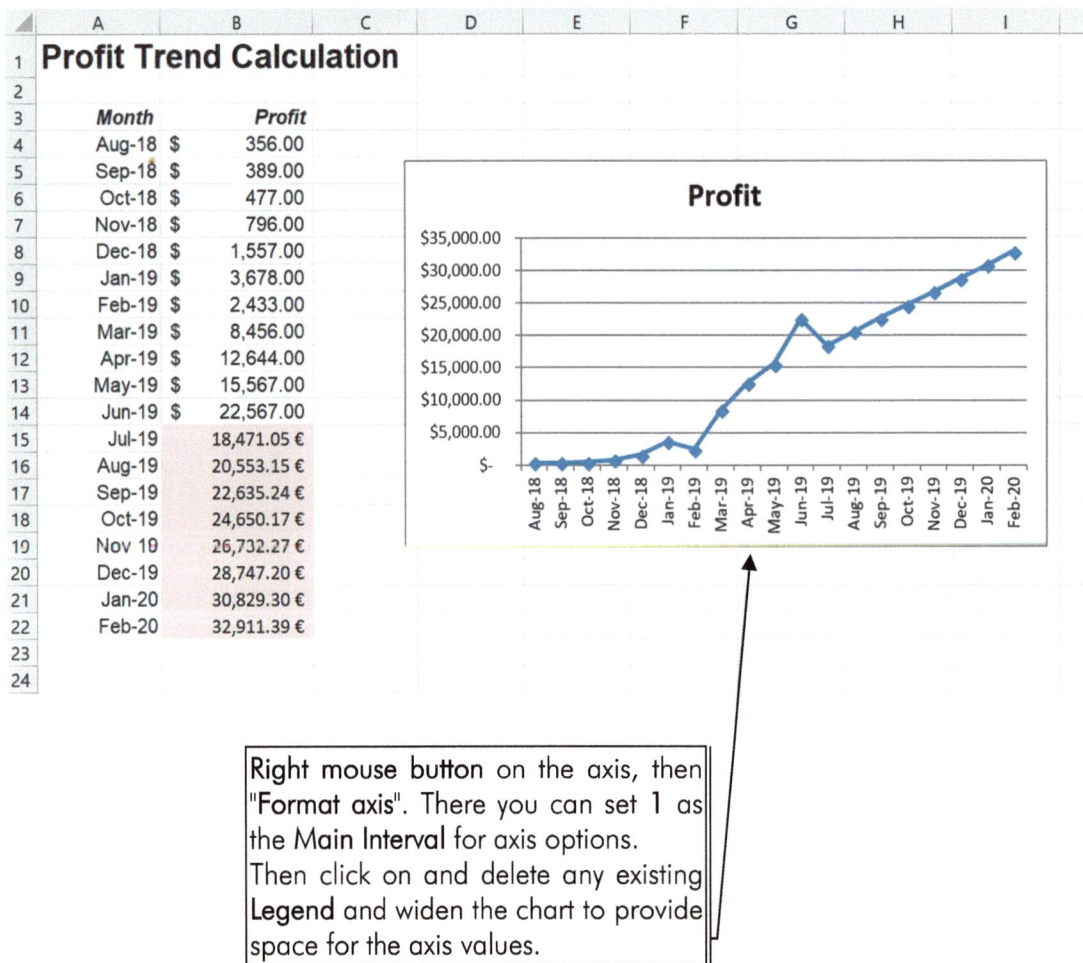

Right mouse button on the axis, then "Format axis". There you can set 1 as the Main Interval for axis options.
Then click on and delete any existing Legend and widen the chart to provide space for the axis values.

18. Pivot Table

This is a function of Excel with the aim of filtering out desired data from large, extensive data collections and presenting it in an appealing way. The X-Y arrangement can also be swapped.

Examples:

- From an extensive database of a butterfly collector, the data is to be displayed sorted by date or genus.

- A company has many branches with numerous sales employees. An extensive table with the sales figures of the sales employees exists. The data should be grouped by store or department or filtered out the top employees on the basis of location.

18.1 Create Exercise Table

An exercise table does not have to be as confusing in length as it's usually the case in practice. For practice, it makes even more sense to keep the amount of data manageable in order to keep track of the effect.

> Create the following **Database**:

Worker	Sales	Branch	Country
Schulz	23.223.445,00 €	Essen	Germany
Meier	12.342.356,00 €	München	Germany
Müller	33.376.778,00 €	Frankfurt	Germany
Hagiwara	13.234.235,00 €	Tokio	Japan
Nguyen	13.452.676,00 €	Hanoi	Vietnam
Schmidt	26.778.456,00 €	Berlin	Germany
de Hulk	87.435.325,00 €	Amsterdam	Netherlands
Stefinski	74.574.563,00 €	Warschau	Poland
Dimitri	75.745.678,00 €	Petersburg	Russia
Wood	24.356.378,00 €	Philadelphia	USA
Spencer	35.346.457,00 €	NY	USA
McDon	23.556.657,00 €	London	GB
Dostojewsky	55.857.643,00 €	Moskau	Russia

> Choose **Insert/Pivot Chart**:

↪ The other option **PivotChart** and **PivotTable** are identical.

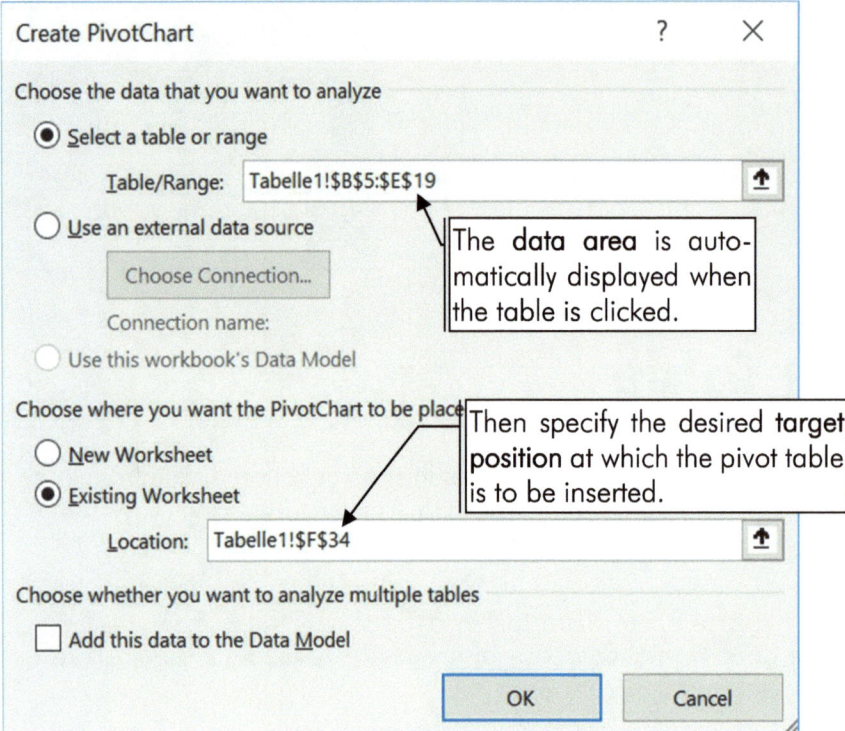

A menu appears on the right, in which the desired fields can now be selected according to which the values are to be grouped:

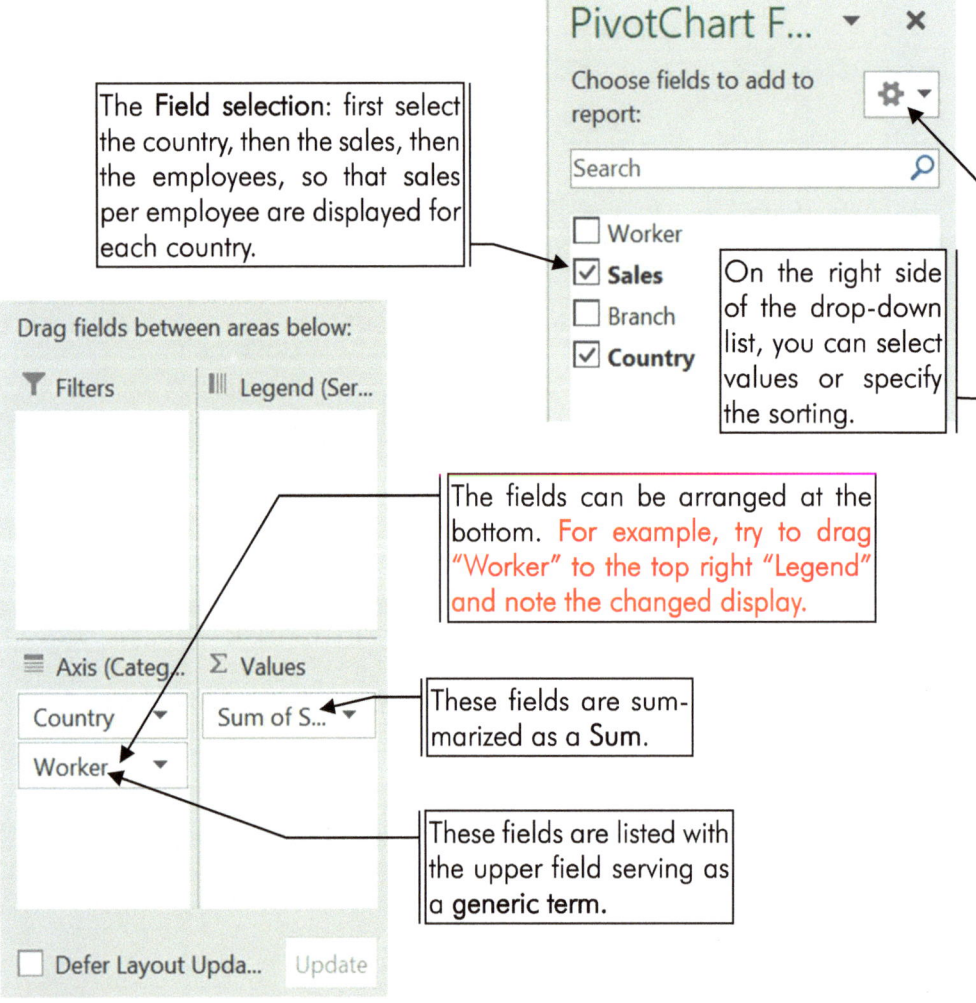

The other fields for the Values selection:

The fields can also be dragged with the mouse from the selection list above into the lower fields that determine the arrangement.

- **Filters**: if you drag a field here, it appears above the pivot table as a filter, and you can select the desired values from its drop-down menu, for instance, to display the sales of some countries.

- **Legend**: if fields are dragged here, their values are displayed in separate columns.

However, we can continue to rearrange the finished table as desired to compile the data as desired, which is one of the great advantages:

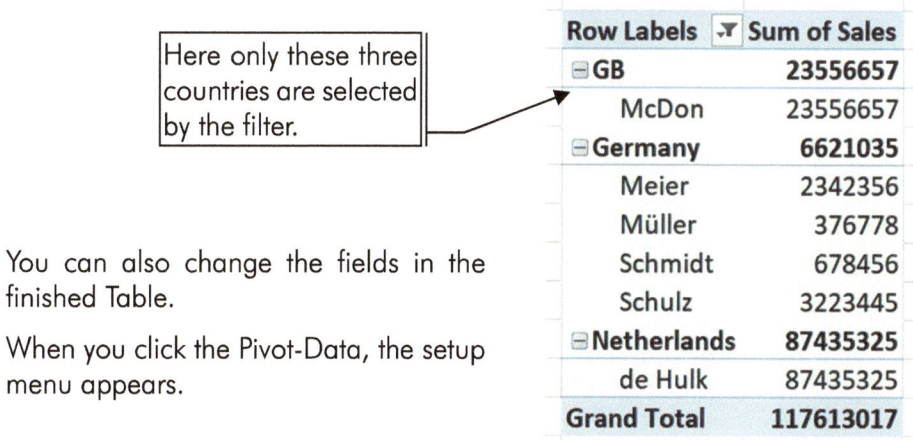

Here only these three countries are selected by the filter.

You can also change the fields in the finished Table.

When you click the Pivot-Data, the setup menu appears.

- Add the second spreadsheet and move the chart there and then zoom in.

- Right mouse button on the chart in order to change the chart type and select, for example, **stacked 3D columns**:

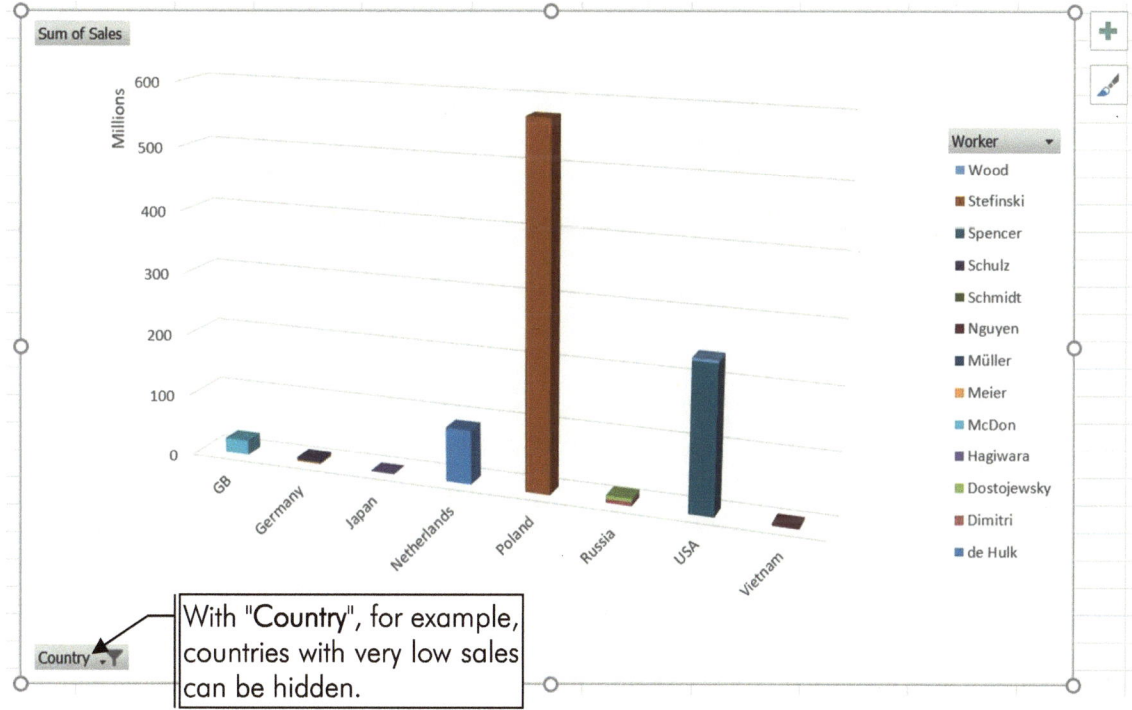

With "**Country**", for example, countries with very low sales can be hidden.

18.2 Overview of Formula Menu

All the Formulas will be found in the Formula assistant *fx*. These can also be found more clearly arranged in main groups on the **Formulas tab**. Whether you want to take formulas from the wizard or formula menu is purely a matter of taste.

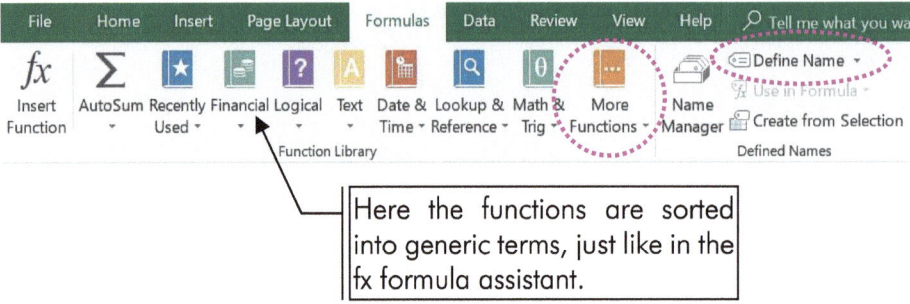

Here the functions are sorted into generic terms, just like in the fx formula assistant.

- Practical: in the drop-down menu of **AutoSum** you will also find the functions **Average, Count Numbers, Max, and Min**. So these functions can be inserted just as easily as the sum in which Excel suggests the above values.

    ✎ The mean value, as well as the largest and smallest value of the sales, can be calculated.

- Under the generic terms such as logical or financial mathematics, you will find a selection and even more functions under the "**More functions**" button.

18.3 Define Names

On the **Formulas tab**, you can still find the name functions on the right side of the Formulas. This allows cells to be assigned names manually or automatically to enable them to be used in formulas instead of cell references.

Let's try this:

> Open the **Grade Evaluation** and select the Grade values H5: H12,

> then "**Define Name**" and enter Grades as the name:

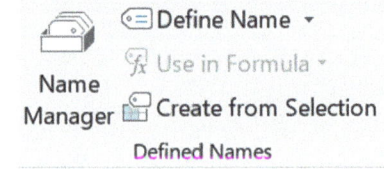

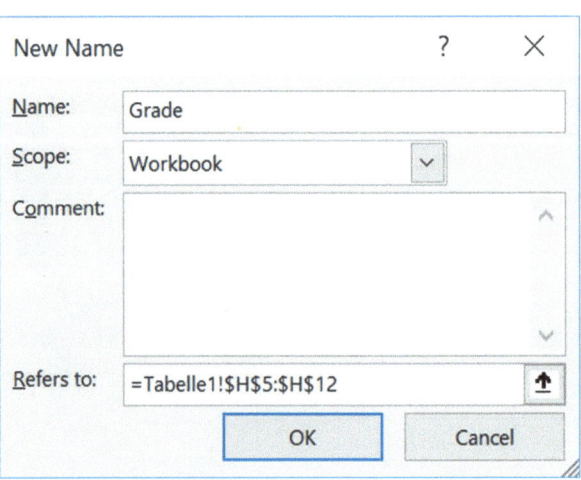

> Now, at the frequency in the formula
> =COUNTIF($H$5:$H$12;B19) instead of the range ($H$5:$H$12) simply enter notes:
> =COUNTIF(grades; B19)

> The formula continues to work even if it is copied down.

Of course, you can also use such names when creating new formulas in the Formula Wizard.

> The naming simplifies extensive calculations and makes them clearer, especially if you work across several spreadsheets.

Other functions regarding naming:

- You can display, rename or delete assigned names in the **name manager**. The values and the origin will also be displayed.

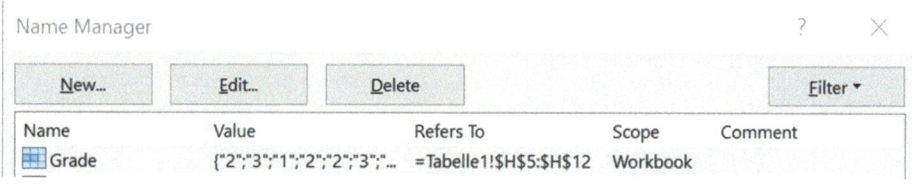

- This opens a window from which the existing names can be selected and thus inserted during **formula entry**. It saves paperwork in case you don't remember the name.

- **Create from Selection:** automatically selects the name.

  - Select the corresponding areas, then select this function and you can choose from the menu that appears whether the name is to be defined from the Heading or other cells:

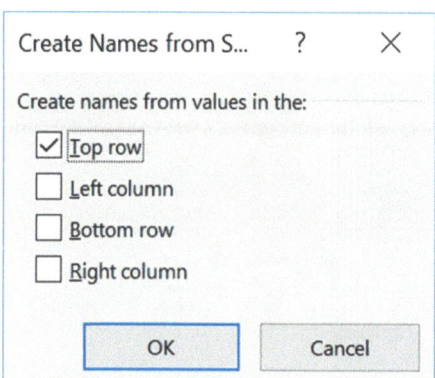

19. External Data, Monitoring

19.1 External Data

You can access data from other workbooks in one workbook. However, the source file may not be renamed or moved subsequently because the data source will not be found or specified manually.

Let's do a little exercise:

> We are using our Grade Analysis. Let's assume that at the end of the school year you want to create the statistical mean of all work to determine in this overview whether the level has improved or deteriorated.

> Open the previous exercise **Grade Distribution** and start a **new folder** in which we want to include this data.

> Type the Headings as shown on the right, then click a cell below it and select the **Average** function from the Statistical category in the *fx* formula wizard.

Statistical Median
1. Test

> Click here, then switch to the Grade evaluation with [Alt]-[Tab] and select the grade column with pressed mouse button at the name list and close the formula wizard with OK.

The following formula is then inserted in the new workbook with reference to the evaluation of Grades:

=MEDIAN('school grade analysis.xlsx'!Grade) - Grade, if defined as name, otherwise ($H$5:$H$12)

In the same way, the mean values of the following school work would be calculated and inserted in this overview; finally, an average value for the whole year could be added.

Specify External Data Source:

- If an external data source is open, you can select the values by clicking **'Show'**. Then Excel takes over the correct entry on your behalf.
  - Either with = the values manually calculate or with the formula assistant which helps to select the correct values for complex formulas.

Some notes on entering external data:

- The file name must be parenthesized [] in square brackets [], or it will automatically be enclosed in brackets when the data is displayed by pointing to values from other tables.
- The spreadsheet must also be indicated, followed by an exclamation mark after which the cell with the data or the matrix must be specified.

Update Data:

- If the entry is correct, you can update or edit the link on the **Data tab** page:

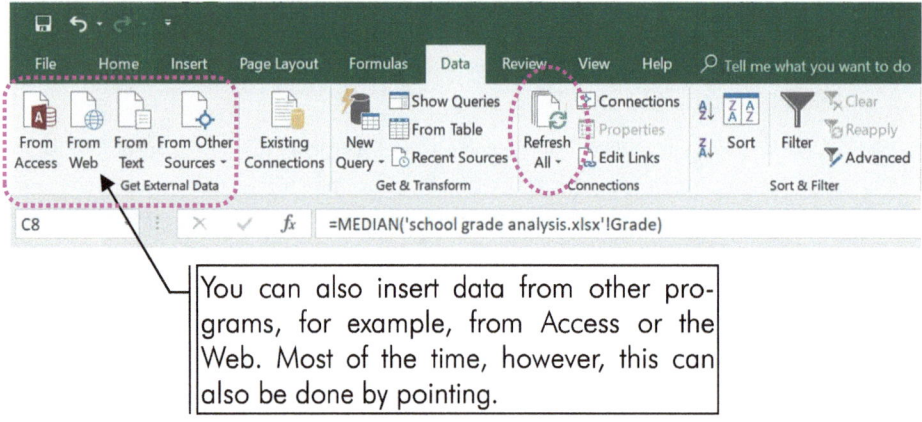

You can also insert data from other programs, for example, from Access or the Web. Most of the time, however, this can also be done by pointing.

- Reduce the size of the windows so that you can see the Grade Evaluation table and the new table next to each other.
- Change a Grade value considerably, for example, by entering only 15 points instead of 55 for Fant.
- The mean value is **updated** automatically.

If an error message appears:

For example, if the source has been changed (different file name or location, etc.), no error message is displayed, but the value simply no longer updates itself.

- Close the Grade evaluation, then open again and change the file name, e.g. add the year.
- Do not change a value. The link to the Grade Evaluation file must be manually repaired.
- Click on Average, then use "**Edit Links**" to open the following window:

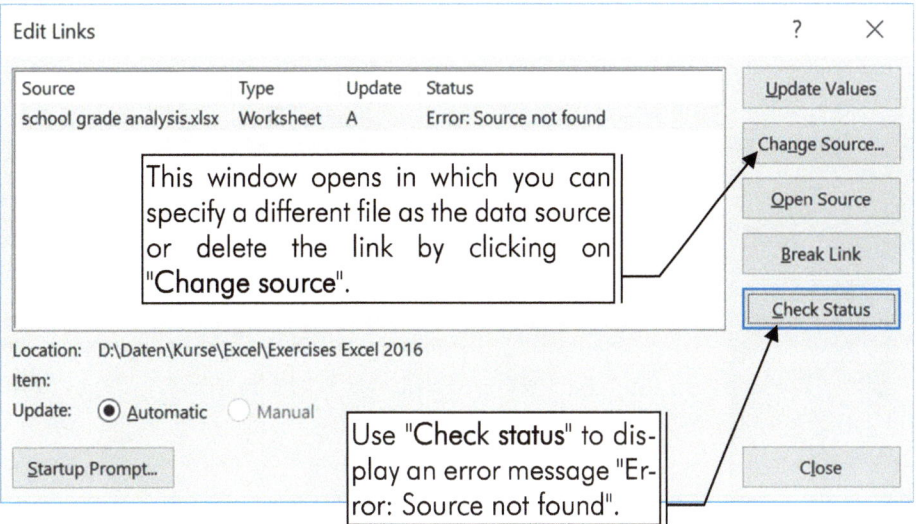

19.2 Hide and Show

It is often a problem with tables that they become too confusing as soon as there are too many columns and rows.

Therefore, Columns or Rows can be **hidden** in Excel.

> ➢ Open the exercise "Travel Expense Accounting...".
> ➢ Select the **Net and VAT** columns and press the right mouse button on the column tab, then select **Hide**.

This column is now neither displayed nor printed and can only be recognized by the double bars of the table tabs or the missing letters:

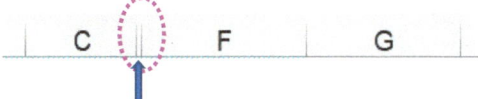

> ➢ **Right Mouse Button/Unhide** can be activated, either press the right mouse button exactly over the two double strokes or
>> ✎ mark the two columns to the left and right of the hidden columns, in this example, select columns C through F because columns D-E have been hidden.

Since you cannot recognize the hidden columns, there is a high risk that when you open the table afterward, you will no longer remember the hidden columns and will overlook them. As a precaution, a **comment** should be set with reference to the hidden column.

♦ In the menu, you will find the commands to hide and show at Home: **Format** (for Cells).

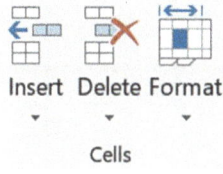

> **Rows** can also be hidden, either by pressing the right mouse button on the left margin or by selecting Mark and using the command for Start Format.

Hide and Show Folders:

- If you select Hide in **View**, you can **hide** the current folder so that it is not displayed. With Show below (open another folder if necessary) you can **retrieve** hidden folders.

Hide and Show Cells:

Seperate Cells or cell ranges can also be hidden by simply formatting them with the color white.

The cells then appear blank; if sheet protection is activated, only the user with the password can make them visible again.

19.3 Formula Monitoring

The **Formulas** tab page contains the commands for formula monitoring which you can use, for example, to display which values are used for the calculation.

> Open the exercise "school grade analysis" and click on a cell at **Grading** that contains a Formula.

> For **Formulas**, you can click on "**Trace Precedents**".

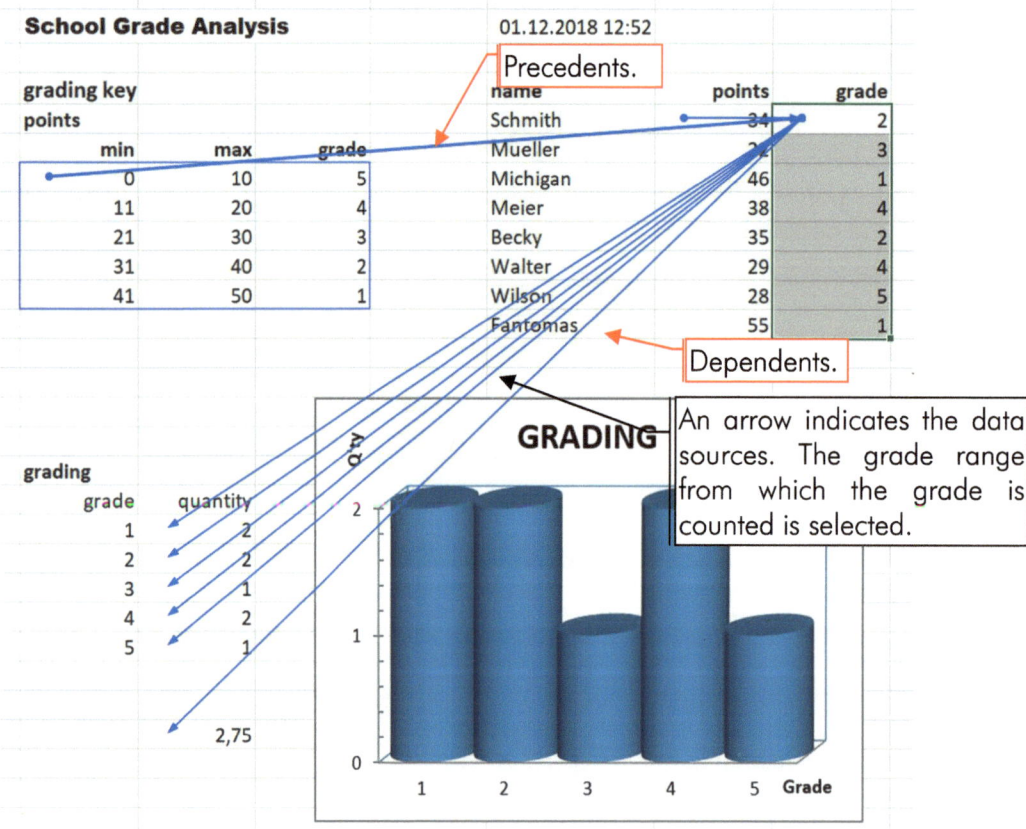

The commands of Formula Monitoring:

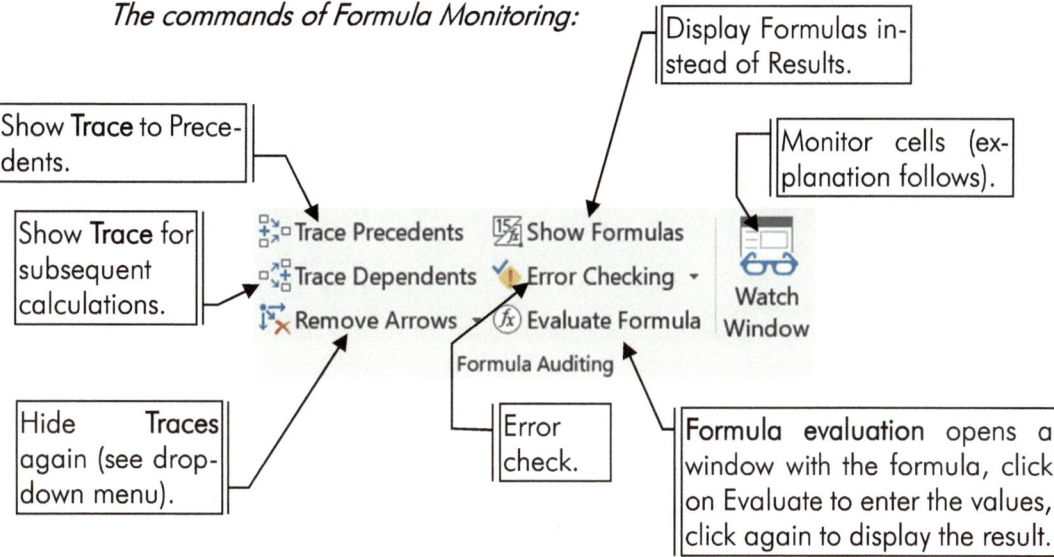

19.4 Monitor Cells

You can use the monitoring window (see above) to display results or values in a separate window. That's all. This is useful for large workbooks while values from other workbooks or sheets can be kept in view.

Click on the Icon to Show or Hide the monitoring window.

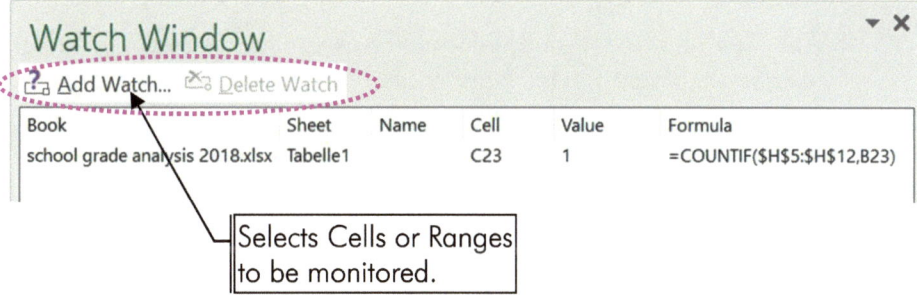

The values are only displayed. If you want to monitor cells in the sense that a message is issued for certain criteria with the validity rules that follow in the next chapter.

19.5 Validation Rules

The validity rules on the Data tab page are used for monitoring in order to report certain criteria. This allows incorrect entries or critical values such as an excessive number of bad grades to be detected.

> In our example of grading, you can select the column with the **Data** obtained and then use the **Data Validation** command on the Data tab to determine that only "**integral numbers**" between **0** and **50 points** are in use.

> Incorrect entries are then reported.

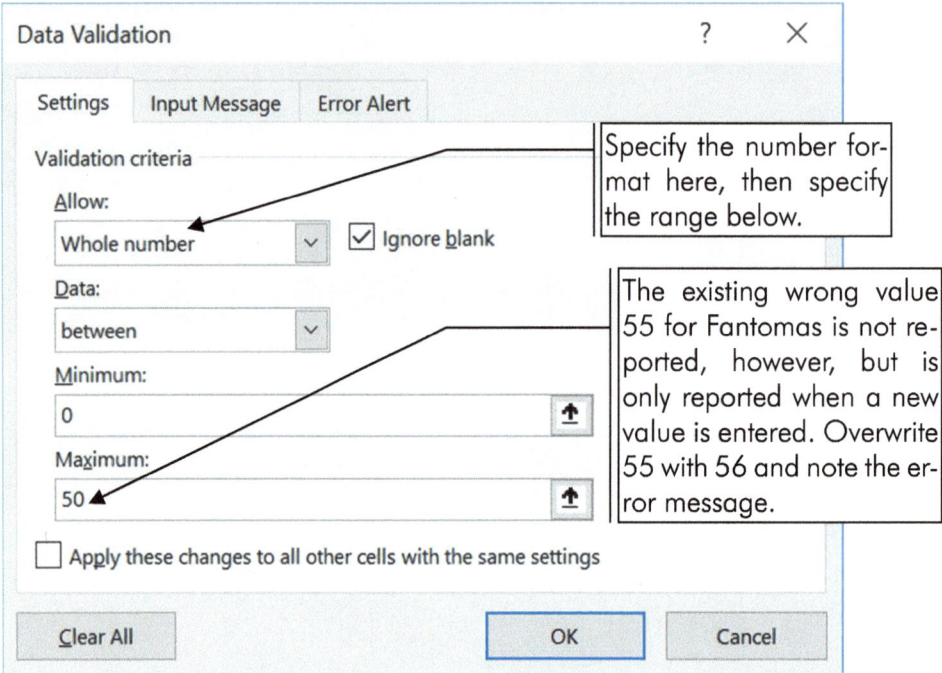

Specify the number format here, then specify the range below.

The existing wrong value 55 for Fantomas is not reported, however, but is only reported when a new value is entered. Overwrite 55 with 56 and note the error message.

More about the Validation Check:

- On the **Input Message** tab, you can enter a **Note text** that is to appear when you click on this cell, also
- on the **Error Alert** tab, a message is displayed when an invalid value has been inserted.
  - ↳ The Type can be selected: **Information**, **Warning** or "**Stop**": incorrect entries are blocked in the latter case.

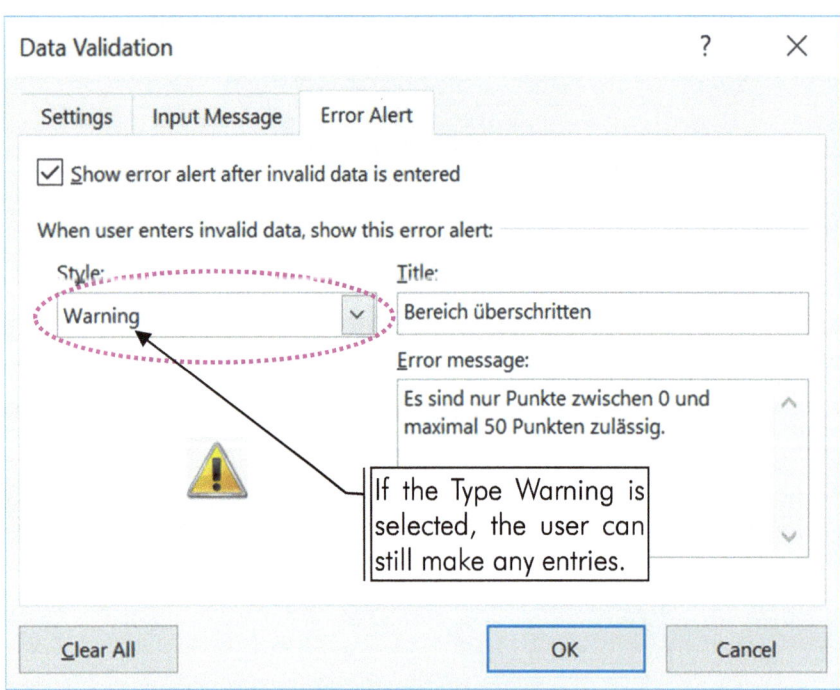

If the Type Warning is selected, the user can still make any entries.

20. Index

&
&Register 32

A
Absolute Relations ..... see Relations
Article 63

B
Budget Planning 65

C
Calculate .... see Formula
Calkulation Program 19
Cell
  -Cell Styles 28
  -Cells Monitoring 129
  -format 39
  -Merge Cells 39
Chart 103–7
ChiQU 50
Column
  -hide 127
  -mark 22
  -modify width 22
  -optimal width 65
  -sort 27
Comment 60, 68
Completion 75
Copy 23, 40
  -Cell 44
  -Data and Formulas 67
  -Format 46
  -Formula 42, 44, 112
  -relative or absolute 44
  -Row 23
  -Symbol 23
  -to another sheet 63
  -Values 23
Correct 11
Count 76
COUNTIF 112
Credit 73
  -End Value 78
  -Formula 79
  -Period 78
  -PMT 77
  -Retention Period 74
  -Template 80
Cube 50
Currency 110
Cut 23

D
Data
  -copy 40
  -Database 50
  -Database Program 19
  -external 125
Date 32
  -Calculations 61
  -input 61
DDB 54
Decimal Place 101
Depreciation 53
Dollar 95
Drawing 88

E
Error Message 102
Excel
  -Extension xls 17
  -start-up 9
Exercise
  -Bonus 113
  -Copy and Move 24
  -Credit 73
  -Currency 110

-Format Transfer 46
-Header and Footer 32
-insert Formula 47
-Invoice 59
-Logic 115
-Numerical Formats 57
-Product 41
-Random Number 51
-Revenues 108
-Salary Calculation 65
-Save 18
-Score Evaluation................... 111
-Series of Experiments 99, 100
-set Formula 42
-Styles 91
-Sum 37
-Tabelle formatieren 28
-Telephone directories 10
-Travel Expense Accounting 110
-Trend 117
-Workbook 21
External Data 125

F

FALSE 115
File 15–18, 15
  -close 17
Fill in 66, 67
Financial Format 95
Folder 15, 16
  -Preset 22
Footer 31, 32
Formatting
  -Format-Table 28
  -Transfer 46
  -with Hide 87
Formula
  -Abbreviation 43
  -AND 115
  -Coordinates 38
  -copy Formula 44
  -COUNTIF 113
  -Credit 74
  -Deviation 99
  -Funktion Wizard 38
  -IF 113, 115
  -in a Formula 113
  -Input 49, 58
  -insert 38
  -Matrix 43
  -Max 99
  -Median 99, 100
  -Menu 122
  -Min 99

-Monitoring 128
-OR 115
-Percentage 59, 73
-PMT 77
-Product 41, 46, 58
-Quantity 76, 99, 113
-Rounding 101
-Show Values 42, 47
-smalles/biggest Value 99
-Sum 37, 38, 42, 43, 47, 58
-Value Added Tax 58
-Variance 99
-VAT 109
-VLOOKUP 111
-with Date 61
Functions 84
Funktion Wizard 38, 49

G

Gaussian 50

H

Header 31
Headline formating 45
Help 26, 51, 84
Hide 87, 127

I

Icons 13
IF-Condition 113
Increment 66

L

Layout 30
Line
  -optimal Height 45
Logic 50, 115
Lotto 50

M

Mark
  -Rows and columns 22
  -Sheets 21
Matrix 44, 111–18

N

Names 122
Note .... see Comment
Number of Pages 32

Numerary 49
Numerary Format 76
Numerical Formats 57

O

Object formatting 89
OR 115

P

Page
- Page Numbers 32
- Setup 30
Paper Format 30
Paste 23
Pivot 119
PMT 77
Pointer 42
Pointing 55
Print 29

Q

Quantity 76, 112
- Sheets 20
Quick Launch toolbar 10

R

RAM 15
Random Number 51
References 43, 44
Relations 112, 117
Relative Relations ...... see Relations
Replacements 44
Rounding 101
Row 22
- count rows 76
- mark 22
- move 23
- new Row 65

S

Salary Calculation 65
Save 15–18, 15
Saving 81
Scroll Bar 32
Sheet
- change 18
Sheets 20, 21, 40

Shortcut
- [Strg]-X, -C, -V 42
Show 127
Show Values 47
Smart Tag 53
Sort 27
Statistics 50
Step value 66
Styles 90, 91–95
SYD 54, 55
Symbol
- Text Symbol Bar 28
Symbols 13

T

Table 20, 33
- format 39
- Styles 90
- to Top/End 32
Table Calculation 19
Time 32
TREND 117
Triangles 102
TRUE 115

U

Undo 26

V

Validation Rules 129
Value Added Tax 58
Values insert 23
VAT 110
View 26
VLOOKUP 111

W

Window arrange 18
Workbook 20, 21

X

xls 17

Z

Zoom 26